Nevertheless, They Persist

How Women Survive, Resist, and Engage to Succeed in
SILICON VALLEY

Nevertheless, They Persist

How Women Survive, Resist, and Engage to Succeed in **SILICON VALLEY**

Nadejda Marques

STONEWALL PRESS
PAVING YOUR WAY TO SUCCESS

Published in the United States of America

ISBN: 978-1-64460-019-1 (*sc*)
         978-1-64460-018-4 (*e*)

Library of Congress Control Number: 2018961681

Published by Stonewall Press
4800 Hampden Lane, Suite 200, Bethesda, MD 20814 USA
1.888.334.0980 | www.stonewallpress.com
1. Social Science
2. Women's Studies
18.12.05

"It is my belief that writers, free-lance authors, should be and must be critics of the society in which *they* live. It is easy enough, and always profitable, to rail away at national enemies beyond the sea, at foreign powers beyond our borders who question the prevailing order. But the moral duty of free writers is to begin *their* work at home; to be a critic of *their* own communities, *their* own countries, *their* own cultures."

—adapted quote from Edward Abbey

Contents

The Faults in Silicon Valley

SILICON VALLEY SITS ON a network of faults literally and figuratively. The Valley is split by the San Andreas Fault, the main fault of the California coastal region, and surrounded by the Calaveras and the Hayward faults to the East and the San Gregorio Fault to the West. It faces the constant and permanent threat of destructive seismic action. This book considers destructive action of another type: that related to patriarchy, sexism, and gender inequality that afflicting an ecosystem that includes the region's premier academic institution—Stanford—and engulfs the tech industry, startups, and venture capital firms.

I take the liberty of using this geological analogy in the preface of this book for three reasons. First, people in the region are no strangers to earthquakes and geological nomenclature. Earthquakes and the possibility of earthquakes are deeply entrenched in the culture of Silicon Valley. Local governments and residents usually have (or should have) prevention strategies and response plans in place in case of an earthquake. In the region, low magnitude quakes are common during "quiet periods" (periods with no earthquake over magnitude 6.0). Similarly, sexism and gender discrimination are not new topics in the region's main industries. Gender discrimination has been well documented in the tech world for decades. During "quiet periods", that is, periods between major scandals or high profile cases of gender based discrimination, instances of micro-aggressions and veiled sexism are common. Only if one of these cases makes national headlines are companies pushed to devote attention and resources to institutional change to advance diversity and inclusion. The changes, however, often appear motivated by legal demands and risk management strategies, thus ensuring limited impact and sustainability. Companies need to do better. They must take comprehensive action to respond and embrace cultural transitions and to develop new socially acceptable practices. Governments, businesses and institutions need to make diversity and inclusion part of all their policies and activities, not only to respond to emergencies but to actively promote sustainable practices and fairness. If they fail, the periods of calm or dormancy they produce will allow frustration to accumulate further. When employees see little progress toward diversity, despite official discourse, they grow frustrated, undermining overall company morale and performance. When reminded of the persistent problems, frustration can erupt in ways companies may not predict. Like earthquakes they can be unpredictable in their timing and magnitude. Still, based on their historical frequency, we can be certain that they will occur.

I came to San Francisco for the first time in 1990 with a student group from my high school in New Mexico. We volunteered at the Salvation Army, sorting out donations, and with other organizations in Chinatown preparing meals to be distributed in community centers to those in need and the homeless. This was only a few months after the 6.9 magnitude earthquake that struck near Loma Prieta peak in the Santa Cruz Mountains, about 60 miles away. The Loma Prieta earthquake took the lives of 63 people and injured more than 3,700. Its devastating impact in San Francisco and on its people was still noticeable and is ingrained in my memory. Many people also remember the Loma Prieta earthquake across the country. The earthquake stopped the World Series between the San Francisco Giants and the Oakland Athletics, the only time in history that the two Bay Area teams met in the fall classic. Because of the World Series, the 1989 earthquake was the first such event to be live broadcast to the U.S. and internationally. Without need of television broadcast, today, innovations and developments taking place in Silicon Valley quickly spread and influence lives all over the world. We live in a time of significant changes when moral values are being re-examined and stereotypical thinking is increasingly scrutinized. Silicon Valley is the symbol of change for the rest of the country and the world. It is a good thing that in the Valley, there are more advocates for diversity and inclusion. The gender gap in tech is a solvable problem. In the past few decades, we have been able to close the gender gap in fields like law and medicine. If we are willing to act and prioritize inclusion, we can close the gender gap in tech as well.

How Silicon Valley deals with the implementation of the ideal of gender and racial equality, as well as how it deals with specific problems of sexual harassment, the gender pay-gap, and other forms of discrimination is likely to set the tone not only for the tech industry as a whole, but also for business and government policies worldwide.

Past frequency of earthquakes and plate motions continually loading strain onto faults help estimate the likelihood of future large earthquakes. Since 1979, there have been four earthquakes of magnitude 6 or greater in the region, leading to the 1989 Loma Prieta earthquake. Based on these estimates and other studies, the San Francisco Bay area is due for a high magnitude quake, possibly the proverbial "Big One". Everyone in Silicon Valley knows it is coming and the risks it poses for its population and businesses. We are very good at estimating economic costs for earthquakes, routinely including them in insurance policies. We are also good at estimating the opportunity cost when women are not included in the economy. However, there are no insurance policies to compensate for losses due to gender inequality. We continue to fail to appreciate the costs that discrimination and exclusion have in terms of building a just society for future generations. Just like the fear of the "Big One," companies dread the day their technology will eventually falter and sink. This day could come sooner rather than later if they fail to include minorities and women. Nevertheless, the contributions that women have made to the development of Silicon Valley as well as changes in its cultural and structural specificities, leaves us hopeful that if there is one place that can make diversity and inclusion work, it is here.

This book seeks to tell perspectives and stories of women in Silicon Valley. As part of the research for this book, I conducted interviews with 100 women to unpack their perspectives and experiences in Silicon Valley, the challenges they face, the opportunities they see, but miss, and the recommendations they give to women hoping to advance their professional careers and personal lives in the region. The women interviewed hold and have held positions in a range of industries, and are from many racial and ethnic backgrounds, and ages. Although some of the women I interviewed held positions of leadership in their fields, I also spoke with women (and men) outside the spotlight. The stories they generously shared presented some overlap, some common trends and patterns but no two answers were exactly the same. I have organized the chapters in this book to reflect the main topics and themes addressed in the interviews. These women's stories have fundamentally expanded my perception of what it means to be a woman today in Silicon Valley. Every interviewee not only revealed important elements of her life but unknowingly helped reveal aspects of my own life. In many ways, my personal narrative resonates with the stories and facts that I relay in this book. My struggles with sexism and abuse, experiences with discrimination, self-doubt, and the failure of people to respect my intellectual capacity are part of a global pattern that is particularly evident in Silicon Valley. The men and women in my Brazilian family are computer programmers and analysts. My stepfather was a pioneer in the field establishing public computer systems in the 1980s and was the president of the first information technology workers union in the country. Yet, I am the one, a Physics-dropout-economist-turned-human-rights-researcher with a public health background who ended up living and working in Silicon Valley. It is with these lenses that I write and understand what happens here. Hopefully, this book will contribute to the understanding of what needs to happen to promote change in Silicon Valley.

Book Outline

This book provides an overview of Silicon Valley's ecosystem, including data on its economic importance as well as accounts of the local culture and ethos. The main premise of this book is the idea that not only can women not afford to be left out of the tech industry, but that tech cannot afford to leave women out. I also challenge the notion that a gender gap problem in Silicon Valley is unrelated from other forms of discrimination, in particular, racism. For this book, I conducted in-depth, semi-structured interviews with one hundred women. Most of the women spoke to me on condition of anonymity that I have extended to all participants. While the names included in the book are pseudonymous, the interviews provide information on personal perceptions of gender issues in Silicon Valley as well as valuable narratives of historical facts and events that took part in the region. The interviews allow for an accessible analysis of the main challenges and potential solutions for an important societal problem.

The first chapter, *On the top of the world*, succinctly introduces the reader to predominant aspects of life in Silicon Valley. It deals with the region's intrinsic contradictions and paradoxes including wealth inequality and cultural tensions. This chapter presents the challenges and the importance of diversity and inclusion not only for the further development of Silicon Valley but also for moral and ethical reasons.

There are deep structural and attitudinal factors that undermine change and gender inclusion in our society. Structural elements are observed in the physical and social environment that includes the educational system. In the second chapter, a *Network of faults*, I analyze how structural elements within the education system affect women's career choices. I explore some of the reasons why important initiatives in elementary and high school to build girls' skills in math and sciences have not translated into robust gains in female participation in STEM (Science, Technology, Engineering and Mathematics) fields at the university level. I also focus on the importance of gender diversity in colleges as a means of providing role models, mentoring, and support networks for women interested in pursuing careers in tech.

In Silicon Valley, Stanford University exerts oversized influence in setting trends for the local culture. This influence might be used to promote women in leadership positions in tech, or not. Every day, throughout their lives, women must confront cultural stereotypes that may or may not align with their technical and leadership skills. In the third chapter *Stanford: the unicorn in the room*, I examine attitudinal forces expressed in beliefs, values and norms that continuously affect women's lives. I also provide some observations on how leadership models are changing to respond to new forms of collective production common in the region.

Women's tech dilemma focuses on the variety of challenges posed by institutional processes that discourage women's careers in tech or even participation in the workforce generally. Despite some institutional changes to promote gender diversity and inclusion in big tech companies, including maternity leave and flexible hours, women are still leaving the industry for reasons that are not fully understood. This chapter offers some hints as to why this is, including a discussion of modern patterns of parenthood that might be influencing women's career decisions.

The work specificities of startups and venture capital firms' operations in the region are addressed in the chapter *Let's talk about money*. My approach suggests that despite recent polarization in addressing gender discrimination against women entrepreneurs, organizing and structuring solutions that include both men and women are important to achieving sustainable, inclusive working environments.

In the chapter *People like us*, I elucidate some of the unpaid and voluntary contributions of women to the Silicon Valley community. Without women's active participation in social and non-profit work, Silicon Valley's divides would be too great to sustain a minimally acceptable environment for its stratified population and would likely erode the political and economic base in which tech companies operate.

Finally, *In their own words*, explains the methods of the study and provides participant demographics and profiles. I also present a sample of the advice given by the women interviewed to illustrate the main themes addressed in the in-depth interviews.

On the Top of the World

AMERICANS NURTURE A KIND of fantasy about California. Before our family relocated from Cambridge, Massachusetts to the Bay Area, we tried to be objective and balance the pros and cons by talking to colleagues, family and friends. "You have to go. You will love the weather." "You have to go, you will love the beach and, oh my gosh, the food…" "You have to go, they are *soooo* laid back." The list of California's wonders was quite extensive but among our friends (none of whom lived in California) the only consensus was that we had to go. Once we moved and were settled in, not far from Stanford, I quickly realized that the place we were in, Silicon Valley, was everything friends told us about California yet entirely different.

The first thing I noticed was booming construction, heavy traffic and constant movement. There was a tremendous influx of people coming to this region, many chasing the *California Dream* of quick fame and wealth. The dream today is not about gold as it was in the late 1840s, but still retains strong emotional and psychological associations with that era[1] such as a general distaste for rules and a focus on raising cash fast. In Silicon Valley, the dream is also about a vision for the future; a vision about where humanity is headed; about using technology to perfect society and human beings while also making millions or, why not, billions of dollars. They call it, the *Silicon Valley Dream,* a name that highlights the place in California where one often feels as if standing on the top of the world. That feeling though is often fleeting.

"I am new to the Bay Area but not new to tech. Moving here was a personal and professional choice. The Bay Area is unique. It is amazing to be here. This is not only a tech hub. There are big tech companies like Amazon and Microsoft that have locations elsewhere. The uniqueness of this place for someone who works in tech is the wealth creation. The differential is in terms of stock options for employees. It is a place where employees own stocks. That is amazing."

—Tendai G., software engineer, Redwood City

The Silicon Valley Dream is not an exaggeration or a leap of faith; it is based on facts and figures. Home to more than 3 million people[2] with reported average annual earnings of $125,580, a per capita income of $86,976,[3] and a poverty line of $117,000 for a family of four,[4] Silicon Valley also houses the headquarters of global tech giants such as Google, Apple, Intel, HP, AMD, Facebook, Cisco, Oracle, and Tesla, to name just the most famous. Together, these companies are worth some $2.8 trillion and account for 6% of all U.S. corporate profits.[5] In 2011, our family moved two blocks from Sand Hill Road, the avenue on the border of Menlo Park and Palo Alto. With its low slung office buildings and parking lots, Sand Hill Road looks like many other suburban California thoroughfares—but appearances can be deceptive. Sand Hill Road is where most of the area's leading Venture Capital (VC) firms are located. This is the epicenter of the mega-region that stretches from San Francisco to San Jose and that raises and distributes some $13 billion a year to startups and select companies. This sum is 42 percent of US total VC investment.[6] It is here that innovative startups from artificial intelligence, biotech, education, transportation, and food processing are created every year. Some of these startups make national headlines, but it is hard to account for all their businesses and activities. In 2017, Silicon Valley listed 31,598 operating startups.[7] This, though, is a conservative estimate that fails to account for all types of startups. Certainly not all these companies are unicorns (companies valued at over $1 billion) nor want to be. Some startups seek no VC funds at all and rely on seed angel funds or even sponsorship by relatives and friends. Thus, the total number of startups and small businesses in the region may be much higher than estimates.[8]

When in most of the U.S. the startup market was still rebounding[9] after the 2008 Great Recession, the San Francisco Bay Area saw 51 new tech startups launched per month.[10] Forget about laid back. Life has a different pace in a startup and around it. People may appear to be laid back (you have to keep up with appearances) but that is only on the surface. It is cool to look laid back but, underneath, people are intense and stressed. Some drink Red Bull for breakfast, protein shakes with phentermine (a substitute amphetamine) for lunch, or simply starve themselves on fasting diets that might last up to eight days. "Work hard but never let them see you sweat," advised one of the first women I met in Menlo Park. To explain this same idea, Stanford students tell you to "be like a duck." That is, be calm and composed on the surface but always paddling madly under the water. It is contagious. When you look around all the things happening in Silicon Valley, anything seems possible. You start asking yourself: If not now, when? If not me, who?

> *"When I was a kid, I used to ride my horse from Palo Alto to Los Altos through Lagunita and the apricot trees on Arastradero. I would ride forever. It was so nice and easy going. You could ride your bike everywhere. School was fun. Junior year was when you could relax, go out on a date. Be back at 11:00PM. Everyone knew each other. It was not about the money at all. When I came back after college, about 17 years ago, I didn't know my neighbors. We say 'hi' but we don't know them."*
>
> —*Melinda H., Palo Alto*

In the Valley, companies and individuals place a lot of emphasis on story-telling their origin and mission; how they have followed their dreams and passions to make an impact and change the world. All that is part of the surface. Underneath, though, regardless of what your passion is, what matters is the bottom line. Everyone is focused and worried about results and productivity. In some businesses, including architecture and design companies, employees receive evaluations every six months. In information technology (IT) companies, employees are evaluated every quarter (perhaps inspired by the Stanford academic calendar also divided into quarters).

The intensity and focus on results is palpable. "It is all about results and productivity all the time," a woman I'll call Kate and who works in sales at Google told me while we were heading to lunch in one of Google's restaurants in Sunnyvale. Big tech companies like Google provide everything their employees might want. They are places of abundance. They provide the best food, transportation and entertainment. But there is a catch. Working hours are long and competition is fierce. Vacations are usually deferred or delayed. These companies also measure everything you do at your work. Employees told me that the companies know how many calls you make, how long you spend on each call, and maybe even where your eyes focus on a computer screen while on that call. With that, and because among their employees there is an expanded awareness about big data, there is a sense of vulnerability and a pervasive feeling that you have to be the best and careful all the time. When you achieve your goals or hit your numbers, companies celebrate to the extreme. They throw parties and make employees feel like rock stars filled with a sense of accomplishment. "That feeling is like a drug. You want to do it again and again" continued Kate, adding that her report was due in a couple of days. Kate was in a good mood and something about her told me she was easily going to hit her numbers that quarter. But others who worked in sales departments of tech companies told me missing goals by even a single digit for a single quarter can feel catastrophic. You didn't give it your all and you let your team down.

"At Google, they expect you to figure things out. It is very engineering oriented. There are lots of folks that don't respect you until you earn their respect. That is the culture. I don't know if it is a gender bias or if it is how they treat the junior people."

—*Sophia L., bioengineer and programmer, San Francisco*

Lindsay is an experienced wellness coach in the region who works with a number of male and female executives and provides services to some of Silicon Valley's big tech companies. She told me that she observed that new employees in those companies often experience a collapse of confidence. "No matter how good you are, when you are at these top companies, you worry about staying on top. But, everyone else around you is also on top of their world. These companies play to our egos and our psychological insecurities," explained Lindsay. The sense of insecurity feeds the competitive environment continuously, with unfounded and racialized arguments. For example, there is an idea in big tech companies that employees recruited from China and India are naturally talented and always good at what they do. Non-Asian employees feel that there is a lot more corporate investment to bring them from abroad, so they "must" be better than the others. The collapse of confidence affects both men and women from all ethnicities but it might be harder for men to give way to those feelings, express themselves or decide to move on and leave the workforce. Society is more judgmental of their choice and men are still expected to provide for their families. The "weaker" link that usually ends up voicing their frustration with the work environment and sometimes giving it up all together is female.

While high in big tech companies, the level of stress is likely higher in smaller companies and startups where there is often a fusion of the private and business spheres. Knowing that some expect less, women in startups feel they have to outperform their male counterparts in every aspect of the business. Lisa, a young woman who lived through this told me what it felt like to her. Lisa has all the credentials to succeed in Silicon Valley. She graduated with honors from Stanford with many athletic accomplishments under her belt. She is a great organizer, a motivated young woman with a strong supportive network of family and friends. After her graduation, Lisa started working in a local IT startup. At first it seemed like a dream come true but with a sunken heart she told me: "It is not easy. The work dynamic makes you do things in ways that you never thought you'd have to… because you constantly need and want to show results." The stress she described took a considerable toll on her wellbeing. To preserve her physical and mental health, she left the Valley. "It isn't fair that men get recreation rooms to blow off steam and women get breastfeeding areas." More than half of the interviewees expressed concern about the impact that the drive for productivity and success has on women's health in general and has had on their own health in particular. Their concern is corroborated by the U.S. Office on Women's Health warning that women are two to four times more likely to suffer from chronic fatigue and other stress related conditions than men.[11]

The Culture

Over time, the name Silicon Valley has become more than a geographical location. At first, it was a reference to the production of specialized computer chips used in PCs, servers, mobile phones and self-driving cars. The association with the manufacturing of chips, however important they may still be, has faded. Today, the name Silicon Valley represents a particular culture that, at its origin and core, is very diverse. Historical factors from the inauguration of Stanford University in 1891 as a coeducational, non-denominational and free institution to the cultural experimentalist climate against the Vietnam War, to the free speech movement and personal expression of the 1960s in Berkeley and San Francisco in particular contributed to create the local ethos. However, a more pragmatic explanation for the local diversity is that many of California's policies, especially those on immigration, favor a diverse and more inclusive environment.[12] Examples of immigration legislation include allowing professional and occupational licensing bodies to accept an individual tax identification number instead of a social security number and prohibiting denial of licenses based on immigration status.[13] These laws allow for undocumented immigrants to obtain driver's licenses and other professional licenses. In 2015, California extended its Medicaid program Medi-Cal to children under 19 ineligible for Medicaid due to their immigration status.[14] In 2017, Governor Jerry Brown signed landmark "sanctuary state" legislation, Senate Bill 54, determining that local law enforcement agents are not required to check immigration status during traffic stops or similar situations.[15] The State also offers in-state tuition to unauthorized immigrant students and has requested action from Congress to suspend deportations of undocumented immigrants with no serious criminal history. And, in 2017, California state lawmakers approved a $45 million budget expansion to support legal services for immigrants.[16]

California immigration legislation and policies have attracted Silicon Valley's greatest asset, its people, and has enabled the concentration of high-tech industries and venture capital firms that wish to draw as much as possible from this broad base of talent, creativity, expertise, and initiative. Silicon Valley has historically benefited significantly from the inflow of out-of-state Americans and immigrants from all over the world. In the past decade, though, the net foreign immigration flow has been consistently higher than net domestic migration.[17] In 2014, nearly one in ten workers in California was an undocumented immigrant.[18] Among tech workers between 25 and 44 years old in particular, 67% are foreign born; 76% of the working women in that age group were born abroad.[19] In two of the three Silicon Valley counties, San Mateo and Santa Clara, over one million residents are foreign born.[20] More than half of Silicon Valley's population speaks another language in addition to English at home.[21] Because of its policies towards immigrants, as well as policies to defend its climate-change agenda and to protect the Affordable Care Act, California is perceived as a progressive and democratic state. Because of its diversity, Silicon Valley is perceived as one of the most democratic and open-minded regions in the state, far more than the rest of the United States—and, often, even more than other countries.

"Coming from South America, I thought this place was very diverse. You have people from many parts of the world. I liked that. But there is an edge. You have to be hip, young and fast. In my line of work, I was used to deeper thoughtful analysis. Here, that was frowned upon. In San Francisco, everything had to be fast even if it was superficial. It was a very different approach and I didn't feel I belonged there in that sense."

—Claudia G., journalist, San Francisco

Silicon Valley has also developed a reputation as an inexhaustible source of creativity and innovation that quickly spread around the world with hundreds of politicians, policy makers and business leaders flocking to it every year to study its secrets and replicate its models of success. Its profound impact on industrial and societal progress is undeniable but there exists in it significant shortcomings and flaws that can be dangerous to its future if they continue to be ignored. Mainstream narratives try to sweep away problems such as strained infrastructure and contemporary socio-economic and technological schisms that the Silicon Valley model accentuates. For instance, in 2017, one in four people in Silicon Valley experienced food insecurity.[22] Some have described this phenomenon of extreme wealth inequality as the Silicon Valley paradox[23] but San Francisco author Rebecca Solnit, using the gold rush era analogy, may provide the best description of the attitudes and culture that allow this contrast between the very well-to-do and the poor. Solnit dubs the phenomenon *frontierism*, an operational style "where people without a lot of attachments come and do things without a lot of concern for their impact, where money moves around pretty casually, and people are ground underfoot equally casually."[24]

Among Silicon Valley's faults are: patriarchy, sexism and gender discrimination. The chronicle of historic facts and individual actors who helped transform a once predominantly agricultural area and a sleepy middle-class college town into a thriving economic ecosystem is nearly, if not exclusively, male dominated.

These common narratives usually highlight the positive progress in Silicon Valley but fail to consider long standing societal challenges such as discrimination based on gender, race, ethnicity, religion, and sexual orientation. In other words, despite its innate diversity, technological progress and economic growth, Silicon Valley has made little progress towards the inclusiveness. Women and minorities have been marginalized from the main industries and held back from achieving leadership positions within Silicon Valley.

> *"The truth is that Silicon Valley is very much like the rest of the country with white men in leadership but Silicon Valley doesn't want to admit that. The talk here is that we value diversity and inclusion. There are some programs here and there but you don't see a lot of change. They can develop artificial intelligence but they can't change behavior? It is not enough to talk about diversity. We'd like to see more than words."*
>
> —*Bianca A., San Jose*

In all, Silicon Valley has created nearly 300,000 new jobs since 2010.[25] Yet, despite this growth many companies have not been able to increase women's labor participation in the region.[26] While most women interviewed for this book agreed that Silicon Valley in general offers more opportunities for women that the rest of the country, they see a general lack of gender inclusion and discrimination in the area compounded by its severity in the Valley's leading industry, technology. This situation undermines not only the fundamental principles of equal opportunity and social justice but also the pool of talent, skills and possibilities from which Silicon Valley's industries draw in the first place.

Of course, there are other industries where women have traditionally been a minority; such as paper manufacturing, mining, fishing, and hunting...But tech is different. Because much of the world is driven by software and because coding is a form of modern literacy, tech holds the potential to be the new, great social equalizer. The tech industry not only offers the best opportunities to create wealth, but also allows individuals to be part of innovations changing our world in ways never seen before. It is not by chance that the word commonly used to describe the transformations tech produces in our lives is *disruption*. Tech disrupts because it is destructive and creative at the same time. It disrupts industries, market places, businesses and our day-to-day lives.[27] Today's tech industries are transforming more than our labor and social relations. They are challenging our concepts of currency, government and policy boundaries. They are also transforming human biology. As futurist author and inventor Ray Kurzweil has observed, technology will determine the evolution of the human species.[28] It should go without saying, but doesn't, that our future as humanity and human beings should not be developed and determined by a single gender; women cannot afford to be left out of tech. Or, more accurately, we cannot afford to leave women out of tech.

Women born in the U.S. have long surpassed men in years of education. It would be unreasonable for tech industries to meet their increasing workforce needs by failing to include this talented pool of potential new hires. Out of pure self-interest, the industry should promote women's work and representation. In addition, research shows that companies with more gender diversity tend to deliver better returns and are less volatile.[29] Greater representation of women can increase work satisfaction, commitment and reduce turnover. Companies with more gender diversity perform better financially than their respective national industry medians.[30] According to the MSCI World Index, in 2015, four of the only seven companies that had predominantly female boards outperformed their industry peers.[31] Companies in the MSCI World Index with strong female leadership generated a 10.1% return on equity per year, compared to 7.4% earned by companies without such female leadership.[32] These results corroborate another global survey that shows that when profitable companies with no female leaders increased female representation to 30%, their net revenue margins increased by 15%.[33] In addition, a Citigroup Inc. study shows that achieving gender equality would produce a 6 percent growth in the national GDP.[34] Companies and the economy as a whole suffer when women are left out of the workforce. In short, gender equality makes good business sense and benefits the whole economy.

> *"When I had my hair straightened, nobody in the office said anything. Then, I decided to cut my hair short and keep it natural. At work my boss and everybody wanted to touch my hair. I know when there is gender discrimination because the men around me receive different treatment. I know when there is racial discrimination when the other women around me get different treatment and I am the only African American in the room."*
>
> —*Thalia M. software engineer, entrepreneur, Santa Clara*

Different accounts suggest that the race gap in Silicon Valley is even worse than the gender gap and that for minority women; race, not gender, is the biggest limiting factor for their careers in tech.[35] Policies to reduce the gender gap in tech cannot ignore conversations and policies to reduce racial inequality. It is not uncommon for the voices of women of color to be excluded from a serious analysis of the historical factors and contexts of power that discriminate and exclude them. Internalization of racism results in feelings of shame, self-hatred and insecurities that exacerbate the gender discrimination. In the U.S., black women are overrepresented in low-paying industries leading to greater job insecurity and lower pay.[36] Given that the majority of women between the ages of 25 to 44 years working in tech jobs in Silicon Valley are foreign born,[37] in addition to barriers to gender inclusion, these women also face barriers related to their immigration status and ethnicity. No wonder, then, that women of color who face both racism and sexism were the first to bring up gender-discrimination cases against tech companies in the region.

"After 20 years of experience in the field, I hit a very difficult point. My boss criticized me for being provocative with my questions and too friendly with the staff. Maybe it was a little bit because I was Latina but I think mostly it was because I was different. They were proud to have a Latina on their staff but it was only for show. I don't know if I was discriminated against because I was a woman or because I am a Latina."

—Rosa C., entrepreneur and educator, Palo Alto.

Better profits and performance also accrue to companies that are ethnically diverse,[38] an important factor in our society that is becoming increasingly more diverse.[39] In the U.S. in the past few decades, the percentage of the population in racial and ethnic minority groups grew among all age groups.[40] The percentage of foreign-born of the population residing in the U.S. increased from 4.7% in 1970 to 13.5% in 2015. This population is more likely to be from racial and ethnic minority groups[41] and estimates are that by 2055, the U.S. will not have a single racial or ethnic majority.[42] A truly disruptive industry cannot afford to miss out on promising solutions or entire markets for its products because it fails to consider diverse voices and perspectives.

Tech industries need representation of both sexes. Despite years of research showing the lack of gender diversity at the top, a lack of urgency for companies to take action continues to prevail. Companies have been mainly motivated by the need for legal compliance and a risk management perspective to take action. However, as Sundar Pichai, CEO at Google, put it, global representation is important but not enough, "technology will render itself irrelevant if it functions in a bubble, to be used only by a few."[43]

Intellectually, Silicon Valley CEOs know the importance of diversity and inclusion. Yet, the women interviewed for this book feel that CEOs must go beyond rhetoric and live up to their promises. Good intentions are not enough. Today, Americans live in a gender-identity and sexual orientation melting pot. Some 50%

of millennials believe that gender is a spectrum and 20% say they are something *other* than strictly straight and cisgender, compared to just 7% of boomers.[44] This variety of identities is reflected in the local companies and the culture at large. For example, Facebook has 51 gender options for users.[45] Tinder, the dating app, has 40 such options.[46] Despite these societal changes and progressive developments, transgender and non-binary people in the U.S. suffer family and peer rejection, employment discrimination, lack of access to appropriate medical care among other forms of discrimination.[47]

Millennials are a generation that pride themselves on values and care about social issues in much greater number than older generations. According to the 2017 Enso's Brand World Value Index, 68% of millennials say they actively pursue their personal goal of changing the world.[48] This leads them to seek to work in companies with values that align with their own. They are also more mobile and unafraid to quit a position if they do not agree with the organization's values or culture. Even if motivated by competition over new talent, CEOs must make gender parity an ultimate goal and establish policies on group representation at meetings, projects, and committees. They set the tone for company culture and have the power to challenge sexism and racism in the workplace. Ultimately, they can and should lead by example publicly and privately, and refuse to be bullies or bystanders to discrimination.

In a place that operates in a five to seven year "relevance" cycle, that is, the time a person remains relevant to a business, ageism, stereotyping and discrimination based on age is also vital concern. Age is not usually what people have in mind when talking about diversity and gender but it should be. In the past few decades, those 55 or older are becoming more numerous in American population. Nevertheless, these individuals remain less likely to be employed than their younger counterparts.[49] There are some important barriers for both men and women to work in tech after a certain age (some informal accounts suggest a desirable age limit of 45-50, others of a cap at the age of 40). Because women are more likely to have interrupted their professional careers, returning or re-entering the labor market later in life, for women 40 or older is often more difficult than for men. This situation poses an interesting contradiction. Many of those interviewed believe that women's professional careers peak later in life, when they have more freedom from their family roles and responsibilities. They are also more mature and proficient in many valuable social and emotional skills yet they are rarely provided corresponding levels of opportunity. The lack of age diversity in work places also creates a lack of institutional memory and enforcement of cultural norms. Since the 1980s, women have been fighting the gender gap in tech industries in Silicon Valley through women's associations and non-profit organizations. With the coming of age of its members, some of these organizations have become dormant but many of their members are still active in the Silicon Valley workforce. The new boom of women's organizations, however, rarely exchanges ideas and experiences with veteran activists in the region. Thus, in many ways, this lack of communication and cooperation between newer and older women's organizations slows the march towards gender inclusion.

As novelist Chimamanda Adichie warned, a single story or a single narrative of events, "robs people of dignity and makes our recognition of equal humanity difficult."[50] In and out of tech, women's work is part of the engine that allows for Silicon Valley's economy to function. Paid or unpaid, women make important contributions to this society. Their stories, aspirations, accomplishments and struggles deserve to be told.

A Network of Faults: How Education is Keeping Women Out of Tech

"When I was younger, I was really good at math. I remember someone told me that I could be an engineer but I said I don't want to solve math problems. Both my parents work in tech and worked in the area for some time but decided to raise me and my sister elsewhere. I think my mom feels that way it was easier to install the values she wanted in my sister and me. Values such as generosity, being grateful, and giving back. When I started studying at Stanford I was very aware of the differences. For instance, during orientation, it was all about you, what you are doing, the impact that you are having, your growth, very individualistic.[…] I got into computer science almost by chance. There is a very popular seminar during freshman year. It was challenging but I enjoyed it. I almost didn't take the following course because a guy in my dorm always finished all the assignments before me. I had never taken computer science before and was never able to finish extra assignments because I was doing other things. Theater and music were also very important to me. I talked to my professor. That conversation gave me a boost. I was doing well in class. She told me: a little bit of a slope makes up a lot for the y intercept. The head TA was a female. My graders were female and were very helpful. Then, I decided to apply to become a TA and I got the position. It was very surprising to me and it made me realize that maybe I'm good at this. I needed this extra validation. It has been tough, really hard sometimes. I definitely struggled even trying to ask a question in class and with colleagues saying condescending things like: this is the way

it is usually done… It is also hard because they value and reward if you devote your time 100% to developing your own app. Those who are able to complete this extra-curricular project also get extra credit that goes into transcripts and translates into more opportunities for internships fast-tracking them into the job they are interested in. People that don't have money or don't have time to do this are at a disadvantage. I don't know a lot of female students doing these extension projects. Your success is tied to the idea that you are willing to devote your entire life to this. God forbid you want to spend time with family or friends or sleep or go on vacation. If you choose otherwise, you have to live with the guilt because they have ingrained in your head that it is your fault. They say: hard work beats talent when talent fails to work hard. And they mean: very hard."

—*Alex S., Stanford University student*

ACCESS TO EDUCATION HAS been one of the traditional barriers to women in tech in the U.S; gender gaps in math start to form in kindergarten. Teachers' expectations in kindergarten that boys are stronger at math than girls even when they perform in similar ways feed on themselves, spreading the gender gap throughout elementary school.[1] A positive attitude toward math is an important determinant of children's achievement in the subject.[2] Despite standardized test results showing that female and male students perform equally well in math[3] and science,[4] gender biases and stereotypes are often reinforced by teachers and peers. Sometimes, gender biases are part of our habitual language expressions that use men and boys as the standard for women and girls. For instance, most people will associate boys to a natural talent in math even from the sentence "girls are as good as boys in math" simply because, grammatically, this sentence establishes one gender as the standard for the other.[5] Language matters. Using sentences that set boys as the standard for girls repeated by well-meaning parents and teachers might have the undesired effect of undermining girls. Instead, for example, we could use a more inclusive sentence such as "boys and girls are equally good at math."

Often, the lack of gender diversity in STEM (Science, Technology, Engineering and Math) jobs is attributed to leaks in the workforce pipeline. However, the leaks begin even before women enter the workforce and one of the largest leaks in the pipeline takes place during high school. In the American high school context, math and science are often subjects for geeks and children of both sexes hide or camouflage their skills to avoid social ostracism from their peers. This situation can be even more damaging for girls retention in STEM classes because while boys are usually encouraged to "toughen up", girls receive cultural clues that no matter how hard they try, science and math are not for them.

In addition to stereotyped roles learned in schools, the efforts of higher socio-economic families to foster young children's abilities through organized activities such as sports, dance and music lessons may reinforce the gendering of their sons and daughters.[6] Gendering among the top percent families may trickle down to other families, exacerbating the gender gap development at early ages. Many women interviewed did not remember math ever being an issue for them as young girls but they recall not wanting to be good at it. I can relate to that experience. As a young girl, I actually enjoyed solving equations and proving mathematical theorems in school. The "problem" was being a girl. Since elementary school, I lived with the assumption that math and sciences were for boys, and technology, a man's job. I, like many others, did not fit in well with the stereotype at school. I remember that whenever we had a math test, I would suddenly be very popular and fellow students seemed to want to sit near me. On most days, however, among my peers, it was not cool for a girl to be smart in math. In my school, smart kids were called names that make "nerd" sound flattering.

Gender stereotype and deeply ingrained cultural biases expressed by the general lack of interest for female STEM role models in schools and curriculum may be influencing girls' K-12 enrollment in math and science courses. Role models serve as an important reference for children's socialization. For example, boys are thought to do worse than girls in elementary schools due to the shortage of male academic role models. Thus, male teachers are usually in high demand in elementary schools. Role models are also important for students contemplating career options and the lack of female role models is one of the reasons women leave STEM fields.[7] Girls should be exposed to a variety of role models to ensure that every girl can find a role model with whom she connects. Throughout history, there has been no shortage of notable and pioneer women scientists but how many can you cite by heart? How many did you learn about when you were in elementary school?

Historically, women scientists have not received credit for their work, or their work has been attributed to their male colleagues. The motto of the OpEd Project, a social venture aimed at increasing the number of women contributing to key commentary forums, brilliantly explains the situation: "Whoever tells the story writes History."[8] Today, women in science and technology are still pushed out of the spotlight. At tech shows, trade conventions, marketing events and other settings, women in the industry are met with indifference or pre-conceived notions that they do not have the intelligence or creativity to make meaningful contributions. For instance, owned and produced by the Consumer Technology Association, CES is the world's largest annual gathering for business technologies. In both 2017 and 2018, CES failed to invite a *single* woman to give one of the several keynote addresses during the event.[9] While women participated in other speaking slots, the lack of women in keynote addresses reinforces the idea that women are not ready for positions of leadership in the industry. These societal attitudes strengthen other negative portrayals of women in media and pop-culture. Despite decades of women's struggle, social and commercial representations of women's roles have not changed much. For those like me, who grew up in the 70s and 80s, the most common female characters in movies and TV shows were longing lovers, damsels-in-distress, persecuted maidens or princesses in peril. Today, some alternative media outlets and online platforms including independent blogs have been providing other narratives and strengthening media diversity but these efforts are still on the fringes of mainstream media. According to the Global Media Monitoring Project, from 2005 to 2015, women's share of news-making roles in the traditional media was only 24%.[10] From 2006 to 2016 (excluding 2011), according to Women in Hollywood, an organization that educates and advocates for gender diversity in the global film industry, in the 900 top films, fewer than one-third of speaking characters were girls or women.[11] Thanks in part to a growing number of women directors and producers and initiatives such as Time's Up and Time's Up Plus One, gradually, women's roles in film and TV are becoming more sophisticated and complex. More prominent female characters in movies and television are starting to redefine our ideas of what it means to be a woman. On the other hand, this is not the case for the women portrayed in advertisements and magazines. Advertisements in particular continue to insist on categorizing women as sexy, simple-minded, silly, helpless, naïve, domesticated, and needy, all attributes that reinforce negative stereotypes held by girls and young women about themselves and make them feel that they do not belong in STEM fields.

To tackle these problems in elementary, middle and high schools, non-governmental organizations (NGOs) and school administrations across the country and in Silicon Valley have started to implement important initiatives to increase the number of girls enrolled in advanced math and computer science courses.[12] Girls Who Code, for instance, provides specific training for teachers and girls to overcome potential barriers in computing classrooms. They also promote the work of women in tech as role models to girls. At Stanford, the Girls Teaching Girls to Code Program provides girls with basic coding skills and introduces them to mentors in the field.[13] After implementing initiatives to increase girls' enrollment in advanced science courses, the Girls Collaborative Project observed that in 2013, girls' enrollment was slightly higher than boys, 22% and 18% respectively.[14] These results are important indicators that we can reduce the gender gap in K-12 education. However, and unfortunately, it is too early to celebrate for two main reasons. First, these initiatives have not produced the same results among blacks, other ethnic minorities and low income students. Black students and Latino(a) students still enroll at lower rates in advanced math and computer science courses—15% and 17%, respectively.[15] The figures from my daughter's high school are indicative of this trend. Exit data for the Menlo-Atherton High School (one of the best public schools in Silicon Valley) show that for the class of 2016, the majority of white students (88%) took at least one advanced class (AP or International Baccalaureate) before graduating compared to just 46.8% of Latino(a) students, 8.3% of African-American students and 11.1% Pacific Islanders.[16] Black and other ethnic minority students face additional barriers that are not necessarily contemplated in the girls in STEM initiatives. Often, these students are given insufficient access to early childhood education. They attend the most segregated schools; are often tracked away from college-preparatory coursework; are often perceived as academically less capable, and are less likely to feel connected to their school environment.[17] All these obstacles and barriers hinder their ability to attend college, develop careers and achieve future success. They may very well be the "Lost Einsteins" as Stanford Professor Raj Chetti and the Equality of Opportunity Project identified, children who excelled in math but are hindered from becoming inventors due to lack of exposure to innovation, socio-economic factors, and their family income.[18]

Because Latino(a) students make up more than half of the California population under the age of 20 and have been the fastest growing ethnic group for the last fifty years,[19] educational inequities affect the *majority* of the children in the state. In effect, the educational system is segregating most of its students and limiting their future options in the workplace and in life. Equity issues that begin in elementary and secondary schools where most minority students are taught by less experienced teachers, have access to fewer advanced courses and poor infrastructure, create the foundation for differences in work opportunity as well as health and wellbeing prospects. When they graduate from high school and consider their higher education options, these students face yet another limiting access barrier: legacy preference. Elite colleges and universities select their student candidates with a series of preferences including priority for the children of alumni. In some colleges, admittance of legacies is four times higher than the general acceptance rate making it harder for minority and low income students.[20] It is not by chance that in 2017, even with affirmative action, representation of Blacks and Hispanic students in American elite colleges is lower than 35 years ago. Black freshmen at American elite schools is 6%; while African Americans comprise 15% of college-age Americans (a gap of nearly 10 points, virtually unchanged since 1980).[21] More Hispanics are attending elite schools, but the increase has not kept pace with Hispanic growth in the college-age population. Latino(a)s represent 22% of college-age Americans yet 13% are at elite schools (a gap of 9 points).[22] In 2012, Black/African American (10%), Hispanic (10%), Asian or Pacific Islander (7%) and Native American (0.6%) combined comprised 35.2% of all the recipients of STEM bachelor degrees.[23]

A second reason for concern is that the positive results in reducing the gender gap in elementary schools and, to some extent, high schools do not continue into higher education. The number of women getting degrees in STEM fields has narrowed in most countries including in the U.S. The biggest decline was in computer science, where women received 18% of the bachelor's degrees awarded in 2014 compared to 24% in 2004.[24] One possible explanation is that while initiatives that focus on building girls and women's technical skills in schools are very important, they must be accompanied by programs and policies to build women's confidence in their technical skills throughout their careers. The baggage of cultural stereotypes does not disappear just because a woman turns a certain age or goes to college. In fact, in colleges, new stereotypes influence women's self-perception and perceptions of other women. For example, stereotypes associated with coders clash with qualities attributed to women. In general, coders are seen as "geeks" or introverts with limited social skills. Women, on the other hand, are often valued for very different social skills, their ability to be caring, sympathetic and friendly. Individual and gender identity as well as group expectations may provide the basis for personal preferences and choices. After years of being told that a woman cannot be smarter than a man or that if she is, she will necessarily be less desirable, it should be no surprise that the "male geek" stereotype for computer scientists has dissuaded many women from considering the field.[25]

While it may be hard to change widely shared cultural stereotypes, it is possible to change the images associated with STEM courses present at schools, universities or any organization interested in increasing women's confidence in tech and leadership. They need to present a more inclusive language, featuring women scientists as role models, and presenting multiple pathways for female success. That is why, in recent years, a number of non-governmental organizations, alternative media including blogs, and social media groups have been focusing on promoting female role-models in STEM. A young Stanford female graduate in engineering I'll call Sarah told me: "whenever I doubted myself, I would surf the web and look up stories from STEMinist to inspire me and give me motivation." Created in 2010, the website STEMinist is one of the new websites that feature profiles of women in STEM fields with tens of thousands followers in social media platforms.[26]

There are also some important efforts for image change at the university level. According to the Clayman-Anita Borg study, Carnegie Mellon University increased the percentage of women majoring in computer science from 7% in 1995 to 42% in 2000 by adopting several strategies, training, and outreach efforts to create a new cultural image in STEM that is inclusive equally for men and women[27] and providing introductory computer science courses accessible to those with no previous experience in programming. For nearly a decade, Harvey Mudd College, in Claremont, California, has been implementing initiatives such as those that place greater emphasis on teaching over research. The College has redesigned its computer science curriculum, and now rewards faculty on the basis of their classroom performance to encourage women to study computer science. These efforts have paid off. In 2016, Harvey Mudd, for the first time, had more women than men graduate with a degree in computer science.[28] Six of the seven department chairs and 38% of its professors were women. That same year, 55% of Harvey Mudd's undergraduate class in computer science was women.[29]

Many universities have since tried to replicate the success of Carnegie Mellon and Harvey Mudd. Stanford's administration has been among those implementing a series of programs to promote women in STEM courses.[30] Jennifer Widom is the current dean of the Stanford School of Engineering and an important role model. The Stanford Graduate School of Business (GSB) organizes several women's circles and specific courses to advance women's leadership. Slowly, we are starting to see some of the expected results from these initiatives. For example, in 2015, for the first time, computer science became the most popular major for female students at Stanford.[31]

> *"In my first job, all the women I knew there had PTSD. We worked for weeks at end, night and day and essentially burn out was very real. I left that job when I started to doubt my skills. We constantly feel like impostors, that we are not that good, that I'm doing something not right. I hear this from directors who were doing phenomenal work. I left at the right time."*
>
> —*Janice N., engineer and product designer, San Francisco*

Despite some important breakthroughs to promote women in STEM courses, engineering professions have the highest turnover of women compared to other professions with nearly 40% of women with engineering degrees either quitting or never entering the profession.[32] The high turnover is an indicator that other important factors in colleges may be influencing women's decisions about STEM classes. Surprisingly, one of these factors could be the very same programs for diversity and inclusion designed to motivate women's participation in STEM fields. Programs that include recruitment and mentorship that highlight the need to increase women participation in STEM fields may be reinforcing the idea that STEM is not for women. That is, excessive emphasis on programs to develop women's skills to increase their participation in STEM might have the unintended effect of signaling to those same women that they inherently lack those very same skills.[33]

It is not uncommon to hear that women tend to be more relationship oriented, more collaborative and better listeners, traits essential in high performing teams and leadership. However, the idea that women somehow should be rewarded because they are more caring, and more nurturing, as professor Barbara Reskin put it, not only diverts men from pursuing these skills but also creates obstacles to women who do not conform to them.[34] We need to understand what Reskin expresses so clearly: the important difference women bring to the table is our second-class status and thus our desire to seek fairness and justice for all.[35]

Another possible explanation is that women are trained from an early age to be cautious and perfect making them more responsive to negative feedback and more fearful of failure than men in many environments. For example, some studies indicate that assessment of learning with an excessive focus on test results may hurt women who already have low levels of confidence. Some women tend to perform worse than men in high-stakes exams but perform better on other forms of knowledge assessment such as written assignments and lab work. Research has also shown that poor grades and large gateway classes are one of the reasons why women interested in pursuing careers in science abandon that path.[36] A celebrated developmental biologist, recipient of the National Medal of Science in 2011, Lucy Shapiro told a Stanford audience, in October 2017, how she always loved chemistry. She told the Stanford audience that because she is also a painter, she could see in her mind compounds in 3-D. However, Lucy got a 'D' in her first organic chemistry class and fell into distress. She started to miss class, tried to drop out and, on her final exam, circled all the option 'B's as her answers.[37] In the end, through persistence and dedication, Lucy was able to prevail. Others, me included, facing similar challenges succumbed to self-doubt and eventually made the decision to follow other paths.

"For one quarter, all my professors were women. It was great! If I asked a question, they did not roll their eyes at me."

—*Sasha A., junior, Stanford University*

In life, people tend to gravitate towards those with whom they perceive some affinity. Some women drop out of STEM courses because there are fewer women in those courses. Exclusion and underrepresentation become a self-perpetrating problem. As one of four women in a class of 60 university students concentrating in Physics in the early 90s, I should know. There was a constant uncomfortable feeling of not belonging due to the casual sexist language and jokes in the room. One of the things that bothered me most was the vulnerability that resulted from my smaller physical frame vis-à-vis my colleagues'. I could not sit in the back of the room and see over the larger male students. I dreaded walking towards the front of the room where I knew all eyes would be on me, scrutinizing my every step.

Female peers positively influence retention of women in STEM majors.[38] Between 2011 and 2015, researchers Nilanjana Dasgupta and Tara Dennehy recruited 150 female engineering students and randomly assigned them to either a female or a male mentor or no mentor at all. Those students assigned to a mentor had monthly meetings to discuss academic problems and develop long-term plans. A year later, the students with female mentors felt more confident about their abilities to overcome academic challenges, and the stress and uncertainty they felt. That is, Dasgupta and Dennehy's research demonstrated that the presence of female peers and mentors can help foster women's aspirations to pursue engineering careers as well as protect feelings of belonging and confidence.[39]

Women's Centers and women's studies programs in U.S. colleges have also been essential to promote empowerment, self-esteem and critical thinking among women. First founded in the 60s, Women's Centers have fundamentally changed the university experience for women addressing and advocating their needs within the academy.[40] Women's studies programs foster personal change contributing to the decline of traditional views of women's roles among college students,[41] as well as curriculum and pedagogical change.[42] The creation of diversity and inclusion programs at the university level, as well as the growth of student organizations and diversity advocacy committees in the past few decades is also likely to reduce traditional interpretation of gender roles. Still, their impact has not yet been fully documented.

Erosion of confidence during college years is also felt when women interact with female teaching assistants and faculty members during their college years.[43] Women are more likely than men to look to teaching assistants, professors, supervisors and advisors to reassure their confidence.[44] Nevertheless, men are the overwhelmingly majority of full professors by rank and many colleges still struggle with acute gender and ethnic imbalance, including Stanford. The women interviewed for this book explained that often white males in academia provide preferential treatment to those more like them while women and minorities experience exclusion and discrimination.

In Silicon Valley, big tech companies are known for hiring the best and brightest in academia. However, this does not explain why top universities in the U.S., including Stanford are disproportionally male-dominated. Of course, there are many women working on university campuses across the country. There are plenty of women who work at Stanford as well. But they are mainly white collar workers and the majority among the university staff and support personnel. It is not uncommon for Stanford and other local companies to hire highly qualified women to serve as receptionists, office assistants and administrative staff. "Offering generous benefits and flexibility is a smart way of getting highly qualified women including women with PhDs to work for less", an anonymous senior female staff at Stanford told me. "For a long time, Stanford has benefited from the work of overqualified women in staff positions that have traded career mobility for generous benefits." In these situations, women make a pragmatic choice about their professional lives, but it can come with a physiological cost. "I don't think I have a professional career. I have a job that I happen to be good at," she added.

> *"I was hired for a position that required a PhD and it turned out to be purely administrative. I felt encouraged by some Stanford faculty members and negotiated my salary but nobody taught me how. They hired me at a very low salary for my position considering the national salary standards. I'm a single mom and the benefits don't make up for the low salary level. I think I should get the salary and the benefits. When I got to Stanford, people told me that it was harder to get hired than accepted as a student at Stanford. So, you walk around with a chip on your shoulder. People who supervised me were men and I noticed that I was treated differently than my male colleagues. They were patronizing as supervisors and accused women of being aggressive when they were being assertive. When there was an opportunity for promotion, I was discouraged from going after it. There is a lack of mothers in leadership positions at Stanford."*
>
> *—Vivian L., Palo Alto*

In academia, men and women hold gender biases that are pervasive. These biases can jeopardize women's prospects of fellowships, lab space, grants for equipment and travel, funding in general, and academic (professional) appointments. In 2017, only 28% of the Stanford faculty was female, and among those that declared their ethnic background, only 2% were Black/African American, 17% Asian and 5% Hispanic/Latino.[45] Based on the academic year 2013-14, women comprise 23% of tenured faculty and 34% of non-tenured faculty.[46] Even in fields that have been traditionally predominantly female such as nursing and public health, men are disproportionately the tenured professors, the department chairs, and the deans. Some students and faculty that spoke to me raised concerns that if demographics were considered only among full tenured faculty in STEM courses, the percentage of women and minority professors would be even smaller. Diversity and representation among faculty is associated with diversity and representation among those receiving doctoral degrees. Data show that in the U.S., women hold 13 to 22 percent of the doctorates in engineering,[47] confirming the interviewees' perception. In fact, a study on the gender gap in promotion to tenure in departments as distinct as Sociology, Computer Science and English, found that differences in productivity explain part of the tenure gender gap but a substantial share of the gender gap remains unexplained.[48] The same study also found that when women receive tenure, it is usually in lower-prestige departments.[49]

Another study found that underrepresentation of women and minorities in doctoral programs is partly due to the discrimination they face as they initiate contact with potential academic mentors and advisors.[50] The same study also found evidence of significantly greater discrimination against women requesting guidance from faculty in private universities as compared to public universities.[51]

Women tend to respond better to positive reinforcement. This leads to problems in academia, where the measure of one's own self-worth is the measure given by colleagues and students. For example, one study found that university student evaluations regardless of the gender of the person evaluating are systematically biased against women instructors.[52] It is particularly hard to build an academic reputation when you and your work are constantly scrutinized through lenses of gender biases and stereotypes by men and women equally.

Gender bias is also reflected in letters of recommendation, writing research papers, access to top publications, earning proper credit for published work, and decisions regarding hiring and promotion.[53] For example, according to UNESCO, women accounted for less than a third (28.8%) of those employed in scientific research and development worldwide.[54] Diversity efforts in academia and elsewhere must be long term investment. But, at Stanford, they seem still to be in an early almost experimental phase, explained a minority female professor who was recently denied tenure at Stanford in a field other than STEM. "There is no tradition of diversity and no reliable form to appeal," she said. In case of appeal, very few tenure candidates receive approval from the provost. One of the best known cases nationally was that of Estelle Freedman, who after 18 months of protests, charges of discrimination and appeals, was granted promotion and tenure.[55] From my personal experience and several conversations with those affiliated with the university, it is evident that there is a discourse of diversity and inclusion at the highest levels yet each department or discipline maintain own interpretations of diversity and often promote it in practice only when convenient or public relation purposes. Stanford employees mentioned that the most visible university policy towards diversity and inclusion is the mandatory harassment training. However, many felt that the training, which can be taken either in person or by watching a training video on a computer, is antiquated and superficial. The harassment training is widely perceived as a purely perfunctory exercise ("to check the box" as one professor told me), thus undermining its reach and legitimacy.

> "It was very hard to attract female postdoc candidates. A wonderful female candidate came and we were showing her around. She was also a young mother and asked to see the lactation room. I was so embarrassed. Our facilities did not have a place to breastfeed. We had a closet with beer cans on one side, a plastic chair and people walking in and out. It was not acceptable. We created the first lactating room in engineering. Before, women were sitting in the bathrooms. Now, we have two lactation rooms. They are beautiful and they have helped us to recruit more women."
>
> —Marcia J. Stanford University

Universities in general, Stanford included, need to expand their diversity and inclusion efforts to post-graduate programs and include on-campus childcare services and support for local public schools. In 2013, 4.8 million college students were raising dependent children. That same year there were 2 million women, college student single mothers.[56] Nearly 50% of African American women attending college are raising dependent children.[57] Childcare in Silicon Valley is very expensive and a great disincentive for women in the region to pursue professional careers. In addition, problematic tenure procedures and requirements can be very challenging for women who are caregivers or those considering motherhood. Speaking about the experience of the Harvard Chan School of Public Health, Professor Meredith Rosenthal explained that women with sufficient qualifications for assistant professor positions are less likely to apply than men with similar qualifications because of work-life balance concerns.[58]

In universities, professors, of course, serve as important role models for college students. Male professors sometimes walk a thin line between intellectual interest toward their female students and sexual harassment. Although strict confidentiality restrictions under Title IX block most campus sexual harassment cases from the public, the most comprehensive research study on the this issue has shown that faculty harassment of students in graduate school is widespread in the U.S. Such harassment includes unwelcome physical contact ranging from hugs, kissing, and serial harassment to rape.[59] Because investigations are often concealed, it is not clear how professors are punished. In some of the more serious cases reported by the media, professors are suspended with or without pay and sometimes allowed to continue teaching.[60] In 2000, Stanford suspended American literature Professor, Jay Fliegelman for sexual misconduct with a young graduate student. Seo-Young "Jenny" Chu, one of Fliegelman's graduate students accused him of rape. She recalled him telling her he controlled her future.[61] The university vice president and general counsel Debra Zumwalt apologized to Chu but the University has not revoked any of the awards Fliegelman's earned in recognition of his teaching. University administration often maintains structures of impunity enjoyed by some professors in even more serious cases. One example is Geoff Marcy who harassed multiple students for more than a decade in different campuses before he was forced out of UC Berkeley. Marcy's departure was driven not by the administration, but by his fellow colleagues and scientists.[62]

> *"It wasn't until my senior year that I had a female professor at Stanford. I got support from female TAs (Teaching Assistants). Before that, I can't think of anyone who was particularly supportive and helpful. When I had female TAs, I felt more comfortable. We worked in teams more often. We worked until late hours but I felt safe. There is a free service on campus that helps you go where you need to go at night. I used that a lot. I think what I saw the most were microaggressions. People making stupid jokes. Once, we had to do a show case on how far we were in our projects. Judges from the industry came to see the projects and give us feedback. My two project partners were female. We dressed up and the first thing one judge said was "when you look like that, I think that you are presenting a dating app. You have to look more like school teachers." I was a bit intimidated and confused. Later, another judge wrote us a nice email to apologize for their colleague's inappropriate comments."*
>
> —*Nicole P., Stanford alumna, Palo Alto*

Women report facing gender stereotyping, isolation and blatant sexual harassment during internships and summer jobs.[63] There are also many accounts of sexual violence and peer-to-peer harassment on campuses. Estimates indicate that for one-in-five women suffer a sexual assault in college.[64] In 2016, 33 rapes were reported at Stanford, an increase from the 25 rape cases a year earlier.[65] By comparison, the city of Palo Alto, in the same year, registered 10 cases of rape.[66] In the first 15 months of the new Title IX adjudication process, Stanford reported 36 cases of prohibited conduct. Of those, eight resulted in hearings, four of which led to findings against the accused. Such findings may result in a one-year suspension from the university, a five-year suspension, or expulsion. Because victims often prefer to stay anonymous, 29 of the complaints resulted in informal interventions that included counseling, group training, and new house assignments. Seven cases received a no-charge decision. In May of 2017, two cases were still awaiting a hearing and five cases were being investigated.[67] Stanford provided the Office for Civil Rights (OCR) of the Department of Education a total of 436 reports of cases of sexual violence and sexual harassment including dating violence and stalking from 2012 to 2016. In 2018, OCR had reviewed at least 174 case files failing to identify any legal violations in the handling of the individual matters by the university.[68]

> *"I decided to apply early to Stanford because I wanted a school that was strong in everything including robotics. I love robotics. I love it here. The community is very supportive and the activities are very engaging. I haven't encountered open gender discrimination but walking in Palo Alto there is catcalling. When I walk alone at night, I don't listen to music. Our robotics meetings end very late, like 3:00AM. One of the moms, when she found out that I was walking alone at night gave me some pepper spray but I don't feel the need to use it."*
>
> —*Emma C. Stanford University*

One of the most high profile cases of campus rape at Stanford involved swimmer Brock Turner who in 2015 raped an unconscious 22-year-old woman near a dumpster outside a fraternity house during a party. The following year, Turner who was indicted on five felony charges was convicted of three felony counts (assault with intent to rape an intoxicated person, sexually penetrating an intoxicated person with a foreign object, and sexually penetrating an unconscious person with a foreign object). The trial judge sentenced Turner to just six months in jail. Turner was released after serving three months of that sentence.[69] Two charges were dropped from his case (rape of an intoxicated person and rape of an unconscious person) because according to California law at the time of his offences, rape could only be committed with the penetration of a penis without consent and in Turner's case there was no DNA evidence to that effect. In 2017, California lawmakers passed a new law updating the definition of rape in the state penal code. California law now defines rape as nonconsensual sexual intercourse without reference to penetration of a penis, accomplished by means of threats, force, or fraud, or with a victim who is unconscious or incapable of consenting.[70]

Sexual violence on campus is a highly sensitive topic at Stanford. The university has adopted new policies to address this including a mandatory Beyond Sex Ed for all first-year undergraduates[71] and an app students can use to report assaults. But students, with whom I talked, feel that the university can do more. The response to the Brock Turner rape is illustrative. Stanford replaced the dumpster and changed the area of the crime with a scenic marker, two benches and a fountain. Stanford planned to install a plaque with a quote from the letter the rape victim known publicly as Emily Doe addressed to Turner. At this writing, the University and Doe's representatives had not agreed on the quote to be used. In 2018, Stanford Law Professor Michele Dauber led a successful campaign to recall Aaron Persky, the judge who sentenced Turner to six months in county jail. The recall campaign petition received enough signatures from Santa Clara County voters to appear on the ballot.

On June 5, 2018, voters dismissed Persky. When universities fail to properly respond to sexual violence cases, it sends signals that reinforce ideas and preconceptions that objectify women or treat them as weak and vulnerable. That is, university actions or lack thereof affect women's individual and collective self-confidence on campuses because self-confidence is shaped by the experiences one has in a certain culture observing predominant attitudes, language and behavior toward oneself or towards those like them. As an anonymous female student protester shouted during Stanford graduation in 2016, "when you hurt one of us, we all hurt."

Stanford: The Unicorn in the Room

"Stanford sets the tone and influences the culture of the Valley but it is complicit in the situation and the problems we have here. There are many aspects to complicity. Pretending that there is no problem is a form of complicity."

—*Rebecca M. software engineer, Palo Alto*

FOR STANFORD UNIVERSITY OPENING Day ceremony, in 1891, Jane Elizabeth Lathrop Stanford wrote a speech that she never delivered. Jane Stanford has always been an important figure at Stanford. Jane and her husband Leland Stanford co-founded the university as a memorial to their only child, Leland Stanford Jr., who died at the age of 15. After her husband died, in 1893, Jane became the sole financial backer of Stanford University and used her influence as a businesswoman to ensure the operation of the university including the hiring of professors.[1] On the margins of her opening day speech, Jane wrote that she did not have the courage to speak that day. Thanks to English Professor Eavan Boland who, in 2016, during the inauguration of Marc Tessier-Lavigne as Stanford new President, read an excerpt from Jane's speech we know what Jane wanted to say.

"I desire to impress upon the minds of each one of these students, male and female, that we have at heart and very closely the hope that you will each strive to place before yourselves a high standard. That you will resolve to go forth from your classrooms, determined in the future to be leaders, that you will live such lives that it will be said of you that you are true to the best that you know."[2]

Silicon Valley would not exist if it weren't for Stanford University. For many years, Stanford has been the engine providing inspiration and setting standards for local businesses and culture. Stanford is much more than a warehouse of brain power providing technical and scientific research for local industry. The university has been instrumental in educating, fostering and supporting entrepreneurs and breakthrough technologies. Like the proverbial elephant in the room, a major issue rarely acknowledged, is the massive, determinative impact that Stanford has on the culture of Silicon Valley. A 5.9 billion[3] enterprise, Stanford is not an ordinary elephant. It is more like the unicorn in the room[4] (a company valued at over one billion dollars) that doesn't get the attention it deserves. In fact, Stanford may well be the first Silicon Valley unicorn. Its power and influence in diversity and inclusion policies deserve more close attention. Stanford could play an influential role well beyond its idyllic campus to promote its stated values. By and large, however, the university has failed to do so.

"Stanford has a strong reputation internationally and in particular in Asia. Stanford has a brilliant faculty and is excellent in research but it is not serving the poor people of Silicon Valley. Where we live, Stanford is a big part of our lives but not a big part of the community. They have this document called message from the founders of the university that there should be no disparity but between Palo Alto, Atherton, Redwood City and East Palo Alto, there is a disparity of 20 years in life expectancy. Our schools are struggling. Stanford could contribute to change that but it is not invested in building community capacity and improving the lives of the communities around it."

—Heather E., lawyer, Menlo Park

When inaugurated, in 1891, disrupting the practices of the time, Stanford University was to be "nonsectarian, co-educational and affordable to produce cultured and useful graduates, and to teach both the traditional liberal arts and the technology and engineering that were already changing America."[5] Its architecture may very well be an example of how Stanford is interconnected and interacts with Silicon Valley's culture. Visitors to the Stanford campus, walking away from the Oval at the end of Palm Drive towards Memorial Church, observe Frederick Law Olmsted's landscape design of interlocked common spaces between gardens that surround Richardsonian Romanesque buildings of local sandstone and red-tiled roofs in the Main Quad. Originally, the many departments were hosted in the buildings distributed around quadrangles that make up the Main Quad. On one extreme, is the History corner and to the other, the Geology corner. Olmsted's idea was that the common areas and gardens would connect the different schools and students could exchange knowledge and work together in those spaces. The rectangular plan of the Main Quad would also provide for expansion of the university in more interconnected quadrangles. One may wonder if his architectural vision was an early influence in the popular open-floor plan promoted to encourage creativity and exchange among employees that became a trend and widely used by Google, Yahoo, eBay, Facebook and other tech giants in the Valley. Many years later, in 2011, Stanford Law School Dean Larry Kramer inaugurated its new edifice, the William H. Neukom Building. Coming full circle, the building, an architectural landmark, is organized around a central open space celebrating Silicon Valley's preference for an open-floor plan and vision of intellectual multidisciplinary openness, ultimately, reinforcing Olmsted's original master plan for the university.

Historically, many of Stanford policies determined the development in Silicon Valley. In 1909, Stanford President David Starr Jordan became one of the first VCs in the region, personally investing in students businesses and enabling, for example, Cyril Elwell, a Stanford Graduate, to create Federal Telegraph, the first major high tech company in Silicon Valley.[6] In 1951, Dean Frederick Terman, who had collaborated with Harvard University in the development of radar countermeasures not only attracted government funding for the electronics development in Silicon Valley but also led the creation of the Stanford Industrial Park (later the Stanford Research Park), where the university leased portions of its land to high-tech firms benefiting from reduced property taxes as well as from businesses in the new industrial park-like setting. Dean Terman would actively push his engineering students to become entrepreneurs. It was under his tenure that experienced professionals and businessmen were invited to continue their studies at Stanford to advance their fields and foster collaborations. The Stanford Industrial Park was the first significant collaboration between the university and tech companies. In recent decades, with government and companies reducing their support and spending of early stage research, university and business collaboration has been essential to maintaining the local economic development.

Stanford has also historically promoted innovation. In 1970, Stanford established the Office of Technology Licensing (OTL) that allows faculty and student inventions to become available for public use through commercialization. The OTL has since generated more than 8,000 inventions, over 3,000 licenses and more than $1.3 billion in revenues for Stanford.[7] Since its founding, directly or indirectly Stanford has supported incubators and accelerator programs that generated some of today's Silicon Valley giants such as Google, Hewlett-Packard, Cisco, Yahoo, LinkedIn, Instagram, Snapchat, all founded by Stanford alumni.[8]

In 2011, a study about Stanford University economic impact via innovation and entrepreneurship revealed that if companies founded by Stanford graduates formed an independent country, its estimated economy would be the tenth largest in the world.[9] Stanford alumni are part of a strong network that recruits, advices and interacts with current students in different capacities. Former Stanford Presidents and Deans such as President John Hennessy as well as Stanford School of Engineering Dean James Plummer, and Graduate School of Business Dean Garth Saloner serve as members of boards in local tech companies including Google/Alphabet, Cisco, Intel, Quick Response Services among others.[10] Intentionally or not, Stanford exerts significant influence in Silicon Valley's culture. For those interviewed with experience studying or working at Stanford this influence is shaped by an important, powerful and conservative institution housed in the most recognizable building on campus: the tower of the Hoover Institution. The very existence of the Hoover Institution with deep ties to the Republican Party and Republican administrations generates tension and potential conflicts of interest with the university's aspirational goal and reputation as a nonpartisan center of higher education. Underrepresentation of women among the Hoover fellows is blatant and not surprising since most of the Institution's leaders have also been members of the Bohemian Club, an all-male club founded in San Francisco in 1872.[11] Some of the Hoover Institution Fellows are unapologetic vocal opponents of affirmative action and diversity efforts sometimes engaging in unorthodox practices. For instance, a recent scandal uncovered efforts by a Stanford-affiliated academic to find dirt on progressive student activists.[12] A young female Stanford student who met with me at the Main Quad, looking at the impressive landmark summed it up: "The Hoover Tower, as pretty as it looks from outside, represents a world of white male supremacy in its crude and explicit form. Just being around it, it weighs on us."

Some of Stanford's notable female alumni include the first woman on the Supreme Court, Sandra Day O'Connor, the first female American astronaut, Sally Ride, former U.S. Ambassador to the UN, Susan Rice, General Motors CEO Mary Barra, the first woman to win the Fields Medal for Outstanding Discoveries in Mathematics, Maryam Mirzakhaniand, and journalist Rachel Maddow. However, apart from CISCO co-founder, Sandy Lerner, and Yahoo CEO Marissa Mayer, there are few female Stanford alumni in leadership positions in the Valley's biggest tech companies. Perhaps this is why over the past 20 years only six women have joined the selective list of Stanford Commencement speakers.[13]

In 2016, at the request of Stanford Provost Etchemerndy, the Task Force on Women and Leadership developed a series of recommendations to improve leadership balance and inclusiveness on campus. The report found that Stanford is not unique amongst top U.S. universities. The study's recommendations were divided into forms to reduce barriers to attaining leadership; nurturing individuals with leadership potential; strengthening inclusiveness processes of leaders; promoting the success of current leaders and ensuring institutional commitment to inclusive leadership through business metrics, accountability and regular reporting.[14] There was no mention, however, of specific measurable actions to be taken in the short run.

The lack of women in leadership positions is a general problem in the U.S. in and out of academia. Despite some recent progress, there are very few women in higher management or on the boards of tech companies.[15] In 2017, while women represented half of all professional jobs, they held only 26, 5.2% of CEO positions in the S&P 500[16] and 20.8% of the board seats.[17] Most of the big tech companies in Silicon Valley are federal contractors and are bound by federal law not to discriminate. They must provide data on gender, age, and take positive measures/steps to promote inclusion. Their numbers on diversity illustrate the scale of the problem and not surprisingly many of the big tech firms are trying to ramp up their efforts.

In 2017, in addition to Susan Wojcicki, CEO of YouTube and her sister, Anne Wojcicki, CEO of genetic testing company 23andMe, high-profile women rose to the number 2 position in many of the largest tech companies in Silicon Valley. These include Sheryl Sandberg at Facebook, Belinda Johnson at Airbnb, Marne Levine, COO at Instagram, Gwynne Shotwell at SpaceX, Safra Catz of Oracle, Ginni Rometty of IBM, and Marissa Mayer at Yahoo. In addition, a number of powerful women executives have achieved to posts in companies worth less than $1billion. However, Silicon Valley is plagued by the leakage of women from STEM. Women don't see a lot of women like them in the tech industry and there is very little career mobility. Stanford Law Professor Deborah Rhode usually warns us that women seem to hit a glass ceiling earlier than we thought. Some of the women interviewed explained this situation by saying that "there is a glass ceiling under the glass ceiling," and the numbers support this perception. For example, while women make up 33 percent of Apple's total workforce and 23 percent of its total technical staffers, its leadership remains mostly white and male. Some 81 percent of its senior officials are men and 82 percent of them are white.[18] In 2016, the percentage of female executives was 26.6% at Facebook, 38.8% at LinkedIn, 20% at Lyft and 12.9% at Google.[19]

Successful women in tech and women in leadership positions are often understood to be exceptions, as possessing attributes not found in most women. In general, people tend to attribute women's success to extreme hard work, help from others or good fortune while men's success is often attributed to skills and talent.

In Silicon Valley, we are told success stories of Larry Page, Steve Jobs, Mark Zuckerberg and other men as if they were superhuman beings. In the rare instances where there is some variation between the characterizations of male tech leaders in the region, they are usually seen as either the brilliant but prickly or the conscious visionary caring figure.[20] The characterization of women tech leaders' styles, however, is heavily influenced by gender stereotypes. Often, women are seen as either not assertive enough or too aggressive. Women who are competent are often perceived by both men and women as cold, unlikeable, or harsh. For example, women are perceived as more likely to apologize than men[21] and apologies are seen as a sign of weakness.

In Silicon Valley the most common terms associated with women in leadership positions vary between *bossy* and the *It* girl. While bossy is self-explanatory, the "It girl" is a stereotyped image of women in tech, in part produced by the media, that attributes added value and gives women celebrity status based on their appearances and not their accomplishments. Focusing on women's appearances makes the case for women in tech even harder. As Anneke Jong observed, while nearly all the top men in tech listed as World Most Powerful People have software engineering backgrounds, among those listed as top women in tech, only a third can code.[22] If you are a brilliant engineer but don't have certain looks, you are not going to be on the cover of magazines, you will not get media attention, you will not be in the public eye much less be considered a leader.

In 2016, a LinkedIn survey asked investors and founders to name an admired leader in tech. 92% of the investors and founders respondents picked a man in the industry. The only woman mentioned in the survey, Sheryl Sandberg, COO of Facebook, was remembered by only slightly over 1% of the respondents.[23] Mostly, these results reflect the male biases towards women but there is also something else at play. Some of the men interviewed for this research reported that when they worked or reported to female bosses, they did not see them as women. They claimed to be gender-blind. Many women I interviewed explained this phenomenon differently. Powerful women executives and female tech leaders in the region were seen as tough leaders that run their lives in ways not accessible to other women. They hardly ever raise gender issues. In addition, many of the women in leadership positions are perceived as fortunate, while they did not have to seek out opportunities, "opportunities came to them" despite them being women. Among these female leaders, avoiding gender issues is not unusual. In male-dominated workplaces, women in high executive positions tend to distance themselves from other women as gender is perceived as an impediment to their personal advancement. In fact, a study published in the *Harvard Business Review* revealed that women and minorities that work promoting diversity are penalized and perceived as incompetent poor performers.[24] This is true in business as well as in academia, Professor Rhode who clerked for Thurgood Marshall before she joined Stanford Law School as the second woman on the faculty, faced several barriers herself before championing women leadership efforts at Stanford. At that time, there were few women in leadership positions at the university and Rhode was counseled not to teach a course on women to avoid being 'tainted' as a feminist.

There are a few exceptions of women in leadership positions in Silicon Valley that speak out about gender issues. One of them is precisely Sheryl Sandberg, the only woman mentioned in the LinkedIn survey. To many women, Sandberg is a model of a highly self-aware leader who successfully demonstrates how company operations interlock with a vision that diversity matters. Sandberg is not only the number two in a powerful tech company; she has also embraced and voiced her female identity in many outlets. She is recognized not only as an admired leader but as an admired *female* leader.

Following the 2013 publication of her book *Lean In*, Sandberg and the Lean In.Org, an initiative of the Sheryl Sandberg and Dave Goldberg Family Foundation, in many ways intentionally and in other ways unintentionally created a new social movement; the *Lean In* movement. With a strong international presence in over 150 countries, the Lean In Circles, groups of women that meet with some regularity to support each other, learn new skills and achieve higher levels of performance in the workplace, have proliferated in the Bay Area. The idea of women's support groups is not new and has gone by different names over the years. For instance, journalist Pamela Ryckman calls the women power circles aimed at helping women advance their careers providing from introductions to clients to advise on perfecting a pitch, the *Stiletto Network*.[25] The Lean In Circles have helped Sandberg concentrate power and media influence around issues of gender inclusion in tech and in the economy as a whole. In fact, in 2018, she was among the first women to ever co-chair a discussion forum during the World Economic Forum's annual meeting in Davos, Switzerland.[26] There have been rumors that the Circles have become cult groups. Nonsense. In 2017, after attending a conference at Stanford, I decided to join one of the Lean In groups. Since then, I have been part of one of the Circles, the Latinas in San Mateo County Lean In Circle under the Lean In Latinas Chapter. Yes, the organizational structure and nomenclature sounds a bit cultish. I had the opportunity to participate in many events, group meetings, and to interview a number of members of the Lean In Circles. The Circles are made of talented, hardworking, smart women (and sometimes men), and it is quite clear that Sandberg started something over which she has little control. Many of the women in and out of the Lean In Circles have been critical of Sandberg's approach to solving the gender gap. "Her approach to empowering women at work is all about autonomous, self-making, self-interested strategies that don't present a vision of the political context of gender inequality around us," told me a fellow Lean In Latina I'll call Elizabeth. It is not clear if Lean In strategies to train women to find ways to succeed in a sexist society avoiding political confrontation or direct challenge to the *status quo* result from Sandberg's self-imposed restrictions as Facebook COO or if they are indeed sincere views on the best means of addressing gender exclusion. A recent Stanford study revealed that women may avoid visibility in the workplace as a pragmatic choice. They understand the career consequences of their actions but on a daily basis they face a reality with very few options. By working behind the scenes, women avoid backlash for being more assertive at work, interpersonal conflict, or feeling inauthentic by emulating behavior viewed as masculine and are able to better make adjustments for a work/life balance.[27] One of the main problems with the Lean In approach is that it asks women to be more assertive and more visible in institutions that are not adapting or creating gender equity. This has a significant toll on women and the unintended consequence of making women feel that inequality is somehow a failure on their part.

To my surprise and to the Lean In women gathered around Market St. and 7th St. on January 20th preparing for the 2018 Women's March in San Francisco, Sandberg made a day-long appearance. She graciously joined and marched with our group, bringing along her immediate family and entourage. Sandberg helped provide polished signs and banners with feel-good apolitical slogans such as "Together we are braver", "Strength, solidarity, sisterhood". She also allowed some Lean In blank signs and posters that read "I march for _____," leaving individual women to carry more political statements if they so desired. It is clear to me that some of the women in the Lean In Circles have not read Sandberg's book but were happy to follow her as one might follow a celebrity. Nevertheless, for the majority of women I interviewed in the Circles, Sandberg is undoubtedly an important role model.

As Elizabeth put it, "she [Sandberg] is not perfect but is one of the best we've got." By addressing gender and diversity issues, Sandberg might have also paved the way for others who follow with their own perspectives. Such is the case of Sara Frier, a former stock analyst for Goldman Sachs and now a chief financial officer for Square, the company disrupting the banking industry with initiatives such as Ladies who Launch.

New Leadership Models

Traditional hierarchies in company leadership are breaking down. CEO credibility is at its lowest level worldwide.[28] To replace them, Silicon Valley organizations have been implementing new models of leadership that are less hierarchical and more fluid exerted more through influence and relationships. The new forms of leadership are more transparent and merge the notions of work and personal lives. These models are fundamentally based on collaboration between companies and the constant need to respond to technological changes. Many companies are striving to become "shape-shifting" companies. "Shape-shifting" organizations can adapt and respond to rapid technological and social-political cycles changes. The relationship between companies is also rapidly changing. It is becoming increasingly common for companies to collaborate *and* compete amongst themselves. When they do this, they are called interconnected companies. As such they form innovation clusters or innovation outposts. The idea of innovation outposts is to monitor development of technology in a specific field to better prepare a company to adopt or adapt to innovations pursued by startups.

Shape-shifting companies and the interconnection of companies push experimentation with co-leadership models that tend to work better for their operation processes.[29] The collective leadership model distributes to employees working in teams or in organizations the responsibility for their work, mistakes and successes. It distributes power and allows individuals to be more accountable, empowered, committed, engaged, creative and innovative in the work they do. The future of leadership is changing or as a female manager in a tech company explained: "Shape-shifting organizations are disrupting our idea of leadership. Honestly, the days are numbered for companies that are based on traditional leadership centered on a few individuals in formal positions of authority."

Collective leadership also works well with crowdsourcing, another already popular work method in the region. Crowdsourcing brings together virtual workers to accomplish tasks and is increasingly being used in various industries in Silicon Valley. To manage teams comprised of online groups of experts in specific fields, from different regions in the world, leadership is more successful when based on an egalitarian model that allows for members to take charge and make changes as the work flows. The new team leaders are those with credibility, authenticity, humility and who quickly adapt to find ways of working collaboratively with others. Team leaders are also temporary positions that last as long as a given project requires. More research needs to be done about these new models of leadership and how they accommodate women and minorities. One concern voiced by long time feminists such as Jo Freeman, is that the lack of formal structures may appear to be more egalitarian and democratic but, in fact, is an unquestioned form of tyranny or hegemony over others.[30] The overall expectation, or more precisely the hope of those interviewed, is that more collective leadership will be more inclusive and more democratic. If so, Silicon Valley's legacy will follow Jane Stanford's wise advice.

Women's Tech Dilemma

"I've worked 20 years in tech. Yes, I have encountered racial and gender discrimination. I have been almost laid off. I have been demoted. At one point, I was getting paid a salary three times lower than my colleagues. I have never been average. I have always been above average and often an exceptional employee, but early in my career, when the company was downsizing, a white man said that I was on the laid off list. He was not being a friend. It was intimidation to make me second guess myself. I had to stand up for myself. I asked him: "why me? I'll sue if I'm on that list and they don't share the reasons." As it turns out, I wasn't on the list. Now that I am more experienced I hear guys saying things like: "I work from 6 to 6" or "you'll need 12 hours to do this." Why is this guy telling me this? They will say that is the norm, the culture; that I have to work 12 hours. Still, I have to stand up for myself and in my head I think: I don't need 12 hours to do this, maybe YOU need 12 hours to do this."

—Tendai G., software engineer, Redwood City

WHEN A WOMAN GRADUATES with a STEM degree, she finds that it is not easy being a woman in tech. More than half of the STEM graduates (52%) drop out of the tech workforce.[1] Confidence, having positive assessment of one's skills and a sense of belonging can affect the level of commitment to and enjoyment of one's profession. A recent study conducted jointly by the Clayman Institute and the Anita Borg Institute for Women in Technology shows that only 37% of women working in tech believed they had the traits and skills of a successful tech worker compared to 56%

of men.[2] This confidence gap affects women not only at the entry level, but in all phases of their careers in STEM fields.

In addition to fostering a lack of confidence, workplace culture influences retention in the tech industry. The women interviewed who work in tech reported a number of factors that contribute to their entry into and departure from the workforce. Among the top reasons are feelings of marginalization from a hostile, macho culture, feeling isolated, stalled, or asked to face extreme work pressures. In the tech industry, the turnover of women and minorities due to negative perceptions of the workplace culture, unfairness, and the lack of opportunity is a $16 billion a year problem.[3] In big or small tech companies women's capabilities are frequently doubted, met with skepticism, categorized as different at best, or inferior at worst.[4] In highly competitive fields, having more education makes women even more likely to experience discrimination at work. According to a Pew Research Center survey, women with a bachelor's degree or higher education report experiencing discrimination at significantly higher rates than women with less education.[5] Another recent study found that 50% of women in STEM jobs say they have experienced discrimination at work.[6] Discrimination at its worst is highlighted by women having to face sexual misconduct that often goes unreported or, when reported, ignored. In 2017, a survey commissioned by Women Who Code found that among 950 individuals who work or worked in tech, 53% of women and 16% of men said they experienced harassment at work. Among the women who reported being harassed, 72% said the harassment was sexist in nature and 45% said the offensive conduct was sexual.[7]

Allegations made in 2017 by engineer Susan Fowler that her complaints of sexual harassment at Uber, the global transportation and technology company based in San Francisco, were routinely dismissed by the company exposed the widespread sexism in Silicon Valley and the indifference of many in the industry to the problem.[8] Multiple employees have since come forward with allegations of harassment and the company has been investigated for 215 cases of sexual misconduct leading to the dismissal of 20 employees for inappropriate behavior.[9] Another case in point, until early in 2017, women working for Tesla, the automaker, energy storage, and solar panel manufacturer, were told to direct their reports of harassment to an ethics hotline which consisted of an automated answering system with no evidence that complaints were investigated.[10]

In general, people struggle to speak truth to power or even to voice their opinions and emotions. We have been acculturated to perceive becoming visually upset or crying as inappropriate expressions of emotions in a business setting while becoming visibly angry and sometimes rude as emotions that are often more acceptable in the same settings. In particular, companies tend to avoid addressing or even discussing issues that might trigger certain emotions such as discontent. For instance, the women who worked at Google that met with me after the infamous Damore memo surfaced arguing that the Silicon Valley gender gap was largely due to biological differences between men and women, were emphatic in their description of how Google handled the situation internally. The measures taken and the ultimate firing of Damore were perceived as damage control measures taken for an outside audience. Internally, almost no one in their departments mentioned or wanted to say a word about it. Mum was the word. One exception was a comment thread shared on LinkedIn in which some women talked about how the memo affected them. The women at Google who talked to me reflected on the consequences of avoiding the tough conversation. They felt that both men and women needed urgent training on healthy modeling for having successful, tough conversations. One of the women put it like this: "People don't know how to have a tough conversation without attacking each other. It's a passive-aggressive culture all around us. Confrontation is to be avoided in the workplace." However, she explained: "Confrontation is important to minimize the damage of bias but companies need to set up a protocol so employees feel safe to speak up in the moment."

Still, the year of 2017 might have been a turning point in Silicon Valley's tech society. Way before the Weinstein cases of sexual harassment made headlines, many Silicon Valley women had come forward with complaints of harassment that led to the resignation of top executives and VCs. Sexual harassment cases were not new in the region, but until recently, women's claims have been routinely discredited. Claims of abuse have been met with hostilities while abusive men have been able to continue operating with impunity, even after repeated accusations of degrading and disrespectful behavior towards women.

> "Early on in my job, I was the only woman on a men's team. I had been working for five years in tech. Customers liked my work but the guys on my team tried to undermine me. They would go to my supervisor and complain about my training materials. They made fun of me and commented on how my body looked to my face. There was a lot of weird stuff going on. They would show up late for meetings and would not give me the things I needed for work. I talked to my manager. They would interrupt me in meetings; make fun of the things I said. After some incidents, I got HR involved. I thought I could work things out. My only regret is that I stayed in that toxic place as long as I did. I wish I had left sooner."
>
> —Michelle Y., software engineer, Menlo Park

In the past, and for some time, women working in tech in Silicon Valley treated harassment as a private matter and carried the weight of sexism individually; only occasionally did they vent with close female friends and colleagues. One woman told me that although harassment made her feel so uncomfortable that she would bring her husband and child to the office when she had to work late, she never filed a complaint. Gradually, things started to change. Women began circulating "watch out" lists that not only included their bad experiences but sometimes named perpetrators of abuse, sexism and discrimination. They shared advice and other information through their networks. More recently, some of the women told me, they used an app called Blind to anonymously talk about their workplace experiences. One woman with decades of experience working in tech who I will call Barbara explained to me: "Before, women did not come forward because they thought nothing would change and that they would be penalized and retaliated against in their companies." She continued, "when you are a victim of abuse and you feel alone, your mind plays tricks on you. You feel shame, fear, and guilt. There is strength in numbers. When you realize that abuse is systematic and that you are not an exception, you start to push for change."

Women started to come forward to publicly voice their experiences of harassment, bullying, and discrimination. Erica Baker, Tracy Chou, Susan Fowler, Whitney Wolfe, Julie Horvath, Sara Kunst, Elle Pao, Cheryl Yeoh and so many others, with help from the press and social media, pushed people to see that sexism is widespread in Silicon Valley. Some of these women took their cases to court and lost; some settled and others won. Individually, coming forward came at a cost to each of them. Together, though, they accomplished something extraordinary. The Uber case is emblematic of some of the transformation taking place. In February 2017, Susan Fowler published a blog post detailing the sexual harassment she suffered at Uber under CEO Travis Kalanick's tenure. Four months later, after investigation, Uber fired 20 employees over reports of sexual harassment, bullying, and other unprofessional conduct. Kalanick resigned. These are not small accomplishments. People began having open conversations about personal accounts of sexual assault and harassment in the workplace, changing how they viewed and responded to those making complaints. Uber's experience with harassment also shows that reputational blowback can be significant, powerful affecting customer loyalty to the brand. More upbeat, Barbara reflected on the year, "For so long, I did nothing about it, people did nothing about it but in 2017 Silicon Valley also had its #MeToo movement and things are beginning to change."

Sexual harassment and violence are major factors affecting women's decisions to join or leave the workforce in tech. If you are a woman and hear the stories of sexual harassment, you think twice about entering this industry. Still, there are other more subtle factors that foster power imbalances and abuse in tech companies. These factors undermine women's confidence, shaping their work-related decisions as well as prospects of gender equality in the industry. To begin, let us analyze the word choice in job posts. People are often unaware that their word choices and phrases can reveal their perceptions and beliefs about gender roles. Word choices are expressions of unconscious biases that have been embedded in our culture and individual psyches. They produce real effects if we don't actively challenge and change them. Job descriptions should only include what is necessary for the position and clarify what skills are expected. Nowadays, job postings must state that the hiring companies are inclusive environments and/or that they are equal opportunity employers. Some tech companies in Silicon Valley are also implementing the Rooney Rule—that you have to interview at least one candidate from a minority group—as hiring policy. These interviews, however, do not guarantee employment since there are no quotas or preferences given to minority candidates. Still, they are a start.

Some of the women interviewed explained how men and women differ when applying for a job. A woman, trying to appear at ease in a job interview is more likely to display calm and even-temperament while interviewers often value displays of excitement. In addition, women also struggle with the Confidence Gap[11] at play in their professional decisions. A woman may be more likely to apply for a job if she feels her experience and skills fulfill all the job requirements while a man will consider applying even if he does not have the required experience and skills for the job. Put aside the fact that required skills may be learned on the job, women often underestimate their skills while men overestimate their abilities.

Confidence is not only an individual characteristic. Research by Textio, an augmented writing platform for effective job listings suggests that the use of certain phrases correlates to a disproportionate number of male applicants.[12] Words and expressions such as "disciplined," "tackle," "work hard, play hard" can be revealing about a company's culture and signal to some prospective applicants that work-life balance might be difficult.[13] By suggesting changes in the language of job postings and replacing terms such as "fast-paced work environment" to "collaborative work environment," Textio's clients have been able to increase the number of female applicants.[14]

Another initiative that is discussed for interviews to avoid biases during the recruiting process is gender-masking. Gender-masking or "blind-hiring" is a process that uses tools such as voice disguiser, virtual reality, or avatars to obscure gender in hiring. This might be a promising strategy. It has been observed that developers tend to accept codes written by women at a higher rate from GitHub, an open source software repository, when they don't know the coder's gender.[15] However, a study about gender-masking revealed that the positive effects of blind-hiring that helped women through the first job screening disappeared once they had to face hiring managers.[16] In addition, these initiatives can send a contradictory message that gender identity needs to be hidden.

Biased behavior can take many forms. Psychologists and behavioral economists have identified dozens of cognitive biases[17] that can undermine women's confidence at work. Those interviewed reported the two common biases they encountered: unconscious biases and social biases. They identified unconscious bias in recruiting, hiring, retention, and promotion. For example, when being recruited, women reported that they felt managers and interviewers, who are often white males, are unprepared for the interviews. These managers sometimes make decisions relying on intuition rather than on candidates' specific skills, capabilities, or experiences for the job. A senior local recruiter who works for the main tech companies in the region told me: "It is not uncommon for managers to be unprepared. They don't have a questioning plan and their questions are usually all over the map." An African American tech engineer told me: "I have two degrees from Stanford but when I go to interviews, I watch the body language and how surprised people act when they find out that I am a tech influencer, I have all the qualifications, and I am a Black woman with curly hair." The tech engineer continued sharply, "they feel I don't belong and more than once they have confused me with administrative or custodial services." This stereotype is reinforced by policies that supposedly are designed to address gender and racial inclusion but focus on hiring women for supportive and administrative roles. Compared to its competitors, Lyft has an above-average level of participation of blacks in its workforce, but, the majority is in administrative support or customer services.[18] In 2016, Facebook, for instance, had 21 times as many women as men in administrative positions.[19]

Unconscious biases can also be exposed during performance reviews and task assignments that require feedback and constructive criticism of female employees. Women are usually penalized more harshly than men for behaviors perceived as "aggressive" and for engaging in office politics. They are labeled "bossy". Women are also penalized for showing emotions in the workplace. Crying in public is seen as a sign of weakness leading women to feel ashamed and alienated by their male colleagues and bosses. Women interviewed related that it is not uncommon for women to cry in the bathrooms of companies like Google and Facebook.

Sometimes managers prefer to criticize employees rather than give praise. Vague feedback is also not productive or helpful for women aspiring to leadership positions. Appropriate feedback is key for professional growth. When employees are not challenged, they are less motivated and feel less connected to the organization. A variant of unconscious bias has also been called second generation bias where sexism operates in ways that seem gender neutral making it hard for women to recognize it and easy for men to dismiss it.

Social biases, even though a bit harder to pinpoint, are equally pervasive at work. When job candidate materials and personal information are made available in a number of ways including on social media, social biases may be at play even before applicants are called for an interview. In the industry, there is a general belief that working with data and writing algorithms comes more naturally for those who are "on the spectrum" or those who have savant syndrome (geniuses with extraordinary abilities to perceive patterns and recall data but, who are socially clumsy). This idea originated in the 1960s when the industry needed to fill out programmer positions quickly and hired psychologists to design psychometric tests to identify "good programmer" traits. Currently, there are numerous psychometric tests, many that follow the Myers-Briggs personality tests and that generally identify good programmers as introverts with limited people skills. Allegedly, Microsoft and Google are among the tech companies that make special efforts to recruit savants or people "on the spectrum."[20] This preference may also accentuate the gender imbalance in these companies as these characteristics are thought to be more common in men than in women.

Another expression of social biases at work is called *sunflower management* which is a tendency to favor harmony over conflict and alignment with the view of leaders. People generally fear being a dissident voice in a company for many reasons including being labeled uncooperative or viewed to be a troublemaker, ticking off the boss, or even being fired. In these environments, the flaws and qualities of CEOs trickle down to other levels of the institution or company thus necessitating even more appropriate behavior in the lead-by-example model for CEOs.

Bias also determines the kinds of jobs offered to women and members of underrepresented groups. When women are hired to work in tech companies, they are usually placed in less-valued positions considered "soft" roles and not highly valued positions such as engineering roles. Traditionally, the workers in tech retail and marketing departments have been much more diverse than those in its leadership ranks or among its engineering employees. For instance, in technical roles at Google, women accounted for 17% of the company's employees with Hispanics making up 2% and African-Americans 1%.[21] Retail employees also tend to be paid significantly less. They are also often not included in challenging projects, nor offered positions such as project coordination, nor placed in sales project management. "Being a project manager in retail is a very stressful position because you need to report results that are out of your full control. Your results depend on other people's performance and you are always on edge controlling budget or clients," related one of the women interviewed. Women working under these circumstances and with the aggravating factor of delayed or slow promotions feel they are stalled, and unable to enjoy their jobs. "I feel that being in a managerial position not only is more stressful, it is a social step down from being an engineer." Some women in this situation used the term *toxic* to describe their working environments. In a toxic workplace, there are unrealistic expectations and responsibilities, discrimination such as underpay, lack of opportunities for progress, condescending attitudes, and favoritism. In these places, women feel that their work is not appreciated or feel disconnected from the organization. Diversity policies in these companies have impacted the entry level-workforce but ultimately there has been very little in actual inclusion.

> *"It's hard for me to know if what I feel is gender discrimination. It could be that people are dismissive because of many things. It could be because I am small, because I am a woman, because I am Indian, because I never dress up. Men walk in the world in a different way. We have to fight for it all the time and men don't. If I'm exhausted at the end of the day and if I'm ill tempered, there is a reason."*
>
> *—Aisha T., lawyer, artist, Berkeley*

As the old adage goes: where there is a problem, there is an opportunity. Because human behavior is subject to measurement, we are able to design public policies that promote gender-equal opportunities. There has been a significant increase in gender scholarship over the past decade. Analytical frameworks are extremely important to produce evidence, identify outcomes and strategies that work, and reveal areas that need to be prioritized. Consulting firms on diversity and inclusion have proliferated in

Silicon Valley. There are online courses, workshops, trainings and new NGOs dedicated to addressing and proposing their solutions to the gender gap problem. While the diversity and inclusion industry is growing rapidly, it is not clear that it has been able to deliver concrete results. Unconscious bias training could become a victim of the "great training robbery"[22] in which companies spend significant resources on leadership training only to find that it does not produce the desired organizational change nor enhanced performance.

Training workers about unconscious bias is helpful to improve short-term behavior but its effects may wear off over time. It is important for companies to promote open conversations and nurture cultures in which everyone feels that they can speak up, take a stand and respectfully confront inappropriate and abusive behavior. Companies must make it clear that harassment, sexual assault and bullying are not acceptable. Companies should also have in place mechanisms to process and investigate complaints. In addition, anti-harassment policies must include corrective action and penalties. With this in mind, Professor Shelley Correll-of Stanford-and her team developed a model that combines three approaches to reduce the negative effects of stereotyping biases and inequality in companies. In addition to bias training, the model includes diagnosing of gender biases in hiring, promotion and other evaluating processes as well as providing specific tools to produce concrete results.[23]

The general perception among those interviewed is that in tech there is very little career mobility and that it takes much longer for women to receive promotions than their male counterparts. This is especially true of women of color. Despite historically having higher levels of education, black women are less likely to move up the ranks in a company and their pay is significantly lower than other groups.[24] More than financial returns, a promotion means the opportunity to try new roles, learn new aptitudes, and to grow personally and professionally. But the gap in advancement is also about the bottom line: salary.

The Salary Gap

"I have been working for almost 20 years. The first time I negotiated my salary was two years ago. It was an ordeal. I felt sick. I contested the terms in the contract and they changed it. I was about to sign a contract that was not good for me. I don't know why. I have read the studies about how women need to negotiate their salaries. I have friends and a husband who give me moral support but still… I was behaving like someone begging for work. I wasn't. They wanted to hire me. The idea of having to negotiate made me sick because I didn't want to be perceived as an aggressive person. But if you don't, they won't ever respect you."

—*Francis L. software engineer, San Mateo*

Women usually accept the salary they are first offered. In 2016, a Glassdoor research project showed that 68% of women and 52% of men; roughly 3 in 5 Americans did not negotiate their salary in their current or most recent job.[25] Salary negotiations are more frequent among younger workers. Of those who negotiated their salaries, men were more successful than women—15% of men compared to only 4% of women—in securing more money.[26] Women who negotiate their salaries or promotions also pay a social price and face challenges that do not apply to men. A woman who works in marketing for a big tech company told me that when trying to negotiate her salary she heard all sorts of excuses and assumptions such as: a women's work is less valuable, that she should be sustained by her husband or simply: "Why don't you move in with your boyfriend? It will save you some money." If she insisted on a salary raise, her manager would tell her: "don't be all dramatic about it!"

Another woman interviewed revealed how after seeing her male colleague request similar performance indicators as herself ask for and receive a promotion during a feedback meeting, she decided to do the same. Her request, however, was met with hostility and admonished. Not only was her promotion denied, but she was criticized for her aggressive attitude. "You can't ask for a promotion, you'll get a promotion when you deserve it." By denying promotion to women, companies place additional hurdles to the development of female leadership and undermine the retention of their female workforce.

In addition to not giving women promotions that keep pace with their male counterparts, Silicon Valley tech giants maintain a gender gap in pay that results from structural inequality to outright discrimination. Given the lack of transparency on compensation structures, we have only a glimpse of the severity of the gender pay gap. Some companies that have contracts with the federal government have requirements and should be compelled to provide pay information to the government but many have not done so or have complied so reluctantly under pressure from activists, the media and stockholders. Google, for instance, is the subject of a US Department of Labor (DOL) investigation into allegations of discrimination against women in pay.[27] In 2017, the DOL conducted an initial audit of Google's 2015 pay figures and found "systematic compensation disparities against women pretty much across the entire workforce."[28] In a statement, Google asserted that its own internal analysis had identified no imbalance. In 2017, three former Google employees, Kelly Ellis, Holly Pease and Kelli Wisuri, argued that lower compensation despite their robust experience and fewer opportunities limited their upward mobility within the company and sought to certify a class action representing all women who had worked at Google since 2013.[29] Again, Google denied the allegations and published a post affirming its commitment to equal pay.[30] Similar class-action gender discrimination suits are pending against Twitter, Microsoft, Uber and Oracle.[31]

Most women interviewed agreed that there is no question that there is a gender pay gap in tech that is increasing over time. In Silicon Valley, the pay gap is greater for women 25 or younger who are paid 29 percent less than men. The gap falls to 5 percent for women 50 or older.[32] Despite decades of equal-pay laws, in many jobs, women still get paid less than men for doing the same work. Why have big tech firms allowed the pay gap to persist? Why are they so secretive about careers and salaries? Many of these firms are advocates for less privacy and more sharing. Yet, they refuse to share their data on diversity and salaries "Where is the transparency?" asked one of the interviewees. She insisted, "Policies in the U.S. seem to be more permissive of wage setting structures that allow for a gender pay gap than some countries in Europe that to promote greater pay transparency allow for anyone's tax returns to be available upon reasonable request."

Sometimes, companies argue that differences in pay are based on previous salary history. However, the Equal Employment Opportunity Commission (EEOC) and several women's rights groups have countered that using prior pay as the sole determinant of salaries perpetuates and institutionalizes the gender pay gap.[33] In a brief about the Aileen Rizo case the EEOC stated: "Because women frequently begin their careers earning lower salaries than men, they remain at a stark disadvantage throughout their working lives. Women who start with lower salaries will continue to earn less than their male counterparts."[34] In October 2017, California's Governor, Jerry Brown signed Law AB168 prohibiting employers public and private from asking "orally or in writing, personally or through an agent" about an applicant's previous pay.[35] The 2017 ban on compensation history inquiries is already being implemented in many states across the U.S. where it is now also unlawful to retaliate against a prospective employee for failing to comply with a wage history request.

Mentorship Programs

"I was very lucky to have had two managers that were women. They were not officially my mentors but seeing them in action was very important for me. I was a note-taker for one of them and it was great to see how she interacted with the team. I learned from watching how she conducted herself in the company. I was an assistant for the second one and she was a great example. I learned a lot just observing how she worked with people."

—Sophia L., bioengineer and computer programmer,
San Francisco

"I hate mentorship programs because they are done incorrectly. It is like... you have a pink shirt, she has a pink shirt; you should be mentor/mentee. Instead, companies could have something like, every Wednesday you need to have lunch with someone different. Mentorship needs to be organic."

—Bianca A., engineer, San Jose

Today, many of the large local tech firms have in place a gender-diversity and inclusion (D&I) program. However, the general perception among those interviewed is that these programs are not well explained within the companies and sometimes result in tensions when men believe that gender policies hurt them. The women interviewed believe that tech companies could do more to train and educate men on how to behave at work as well as being instructed on the purpose of D&I programs. Organizations know they need to minimize differences in progression into positions of leadership. To this end, some tech companies offer supporting programs for women in leadership positions by providing mentorship and social support such as focus groups. However, research shows that only one in four women feel they have personally benefited from these gender-diversity supporting initiatives.[36] When relationships are forced and mentorship programs are not organic, participating in such programs often generates feelings of guilt and dissatisfaction. The research literature shows that sponsorship programs tend to work better to promote the advancement of women in the workplace than mentorships. Often, one needs to be aware of a mentor's biases and motivations. Cross-racial comfort levels can influence the quality of interactions and feedback provided in mentorship programs. Sometimes, mentors lack the time or interest to understand their mentee's needs. And lack of knowledge about the mentee's background and context may result in advice that is not relevant. One young programmer told me, "You can't rely on only one person. You need to have a group of people, your personal board of directors, made of people you know and it would be even better if they are not appointed by your company. You need to feel comfortable to ask them for advice depending on your specific needs."

Pregnancy and the Motherhood Penalty

Tech companies usually associate performance with organizational culture. Employees are expected to be in the office for work, to go out for company happy hour, to attend wine-tasting parties, to go on company trips, and participate in other activities that can be time-consuming for those hoping to start a family or who must care for others. The biases mentioned above and the pay differentials are accentuated when a woman becomes pregnant. While fatherhood is considered a "bonus" for most men, signaling stability and deservingness, the perceptions and expectations of motherhood are linked to the idea that a woman is less committed to her work. This is also known as the motherhood penalty. Michelle J. Budig, a professor at the University of Massachusetts-Amherst, further clarifies that these expectations vary according to income and social class levels. The fatherhood bonus is greater for men at the top of the salary levels. The motherhood penalty, on the other hand, is disproportionally greater at the bottom of the income distribution, especially among those who can least afford it.[37]

Most of the women interviewed praised the family benefits provided by large tech companies such as Google and Facebook. Other companies in the region, though, have been slow to offer flexible working conditions, family-friendly policies, or longer parental leaves for both women and men. Child care in the workplace or even in the co-work spaces is rare. When childcare services are available, they are very expensive (about $2,000 per month). A woman told me how she joined a fitness center not for the workout lessons, but to make use of their drop-in childcare services whenever she needed to go for a work meeting. Local schools increasingly are adopting shorter class schedules that change often and do not follow or easily adapt to regular business hours. Often, families with children need to organize their work schedule around the child's school and out-of-school activities or have a parent at home, usually the mother. It is thus no surprise that among those women interviewed caregiving is one of the main reasons for leaving and remaining out of the workforce.[38]

"I made a selfish decision to keep working and had a lot of help along the way. I did not understand why, in a private school, in addition to paying the bills I was also expected to be baking goods for their fairs and events. I am a doctor and work for a VC company. I didn't appreciate that motherhood was evaluated by the goodies I didn't bake."

—Shalani D., Palo Alto

Some women I interviewed also reported instances of bullying and discrimination due to pregnancy. Lola, a Latina working in tech told me how when she mentioned to her company mentor that she was interested in having a baby, her mentor strongly opposed the idea: "Don't do that," he told her. "Pregnancy discrimination is not uncommon. Managers tend to be more reluctant to promote a woman if she is contemplating family plans," concluded Lola. In fact, pregnancy discrimination can reach absurd extremes: women reported being discriminated against in a genetic testing company that performs pregnancy tests. This was the case of Melissa Blain Johnson, a former employee of Natera, a company based in San Jose, who sued the company for discrimination based on her gender and because of her pregnancy.

"I regret telling people I was pregnant. So much so that during my second pregnancy, I didn't tell anyone until I was seven months pregnant. I want to share this story with you because I know my ability to work did not change with pregnancy and it is unfortunate that in this day and age, we have to feel otherwise."

—Martha R., software engineer, Santa Clara

Overall, for those working in large tech companies, maternity leave is a double-edged sword. If leave policies are short, women may leave the workforce because they cannot afford or don't want to leave their babies behind; if leaves are long (over six months), women fear that their skills will become rusty and they will constantly have to catch up with their peers. "I was afraid that during my maternity leave they would come up with a new computer language. I even had nightmares about it," a software engineer told me. In general, women interviewed worried that the combination of intense competition or "sharp-elbows syndrome" and the apparent work location flexibility for mothers result in pressure to work from home, putting in even more hours than if they were working on the company's site. There is greater flexibility today and women can work remotely. But the same technology that allowed that flexibility is a source of constant stress. One of the women interviewed, a mother of two explained: "The possibility of working from home is also the impossibility of not working from home. I would get emails from my boss at around 11:00 PM and felt the urge to reply right away."

> *"Both my husband and I were working in high tech when we moved here. I was a manager and had to travel for work. I was getting sad because I wanted to spend more time with my kids. I had a 2 and a 4 year old. When I got pregnant with my third child, I asked my company for some time to take care of the transition but they offered me two weeks. I took an eight year break."*
>
> —*Ursula R, Palo Alto*

The Gig Economy

There is also another very important concern raised by interviewees. Many tech companies in the region are increasingly using a vast and diffuse force of independent contractors, freelance coders, and designers. From 2005 to 2015, net job growth has been driven by the gig economy—sometimes referred as the "contingent workforce".[39] If you have worked as a temp, freelancer, contract worker or casual employee—congratulations, you are part of the "Gig Economy". Funny how concepts get appropriated and their meanings reversed. The term "gig" comes from the jazz scene where musicians had to make a living by going from club to club, sometimes in different parts of the country. Today, the idea of uncertainty or unpredictability has been flipped and sold as a lifestyle choice preference for independence and autonomy. In practice, however, these jobs seldom offer guarantees or benefits such as overtime compensation, vacation or health insurance.

The Great Recession and Silicon Valley's extremely high cost of living also push more people into working part-time for economic reasons.[40] A family in the area might earn a 6 digit income, but still feel that it is not enough. As a result, in many families, women who left the workforce to care for family members must still supplement the household income despite family obligations. Because they are usually trying to balance life-commitments and work, they end up favoring work and jobs that are flexible in nature, part-time, temporary or casual work, precisely what we defined earlier as the gig economy. Needless to say, part-time jobs are often downgraded and perceived as less senior. One indirect consequence of the gig economy for women is that they become even more dependent financially on their spouses, reaffirming the cost-benefit analysis that originally favored the man's career over the woman's. There is an expectation that women should work as much as men even though women get paid less and do more household work. Women in this situation are constantly changing jobs and careers. Like almost everything in the Valley, there is a term for it: *pivoting*. Those interviewed who could be considered part of the contingent workforce reported that they felt less valued by their employers and were not satisfied with their jobs due to lack of benefits and guarantees.

The gender pay gap is also present in the gig economy even if not directly related to discrimination. A survey by Bankrate. com suggests that men's earnings from gigs are almost three times higher than women's. In part, this is due to the kinds of freelance jobs that men and women choose. While men are more likely to engage in manual labor such as repair and maintenance work that are more lucrative, women are more likely to provide services as babysitters or caregivers that are comparatively less lucrative. Even when both men and women engage in the same work such as financial advising or as Uber drivers, for instance, women tend to earn less than men.[41]

In addition, these employees are not fully protected by the law. They have signed arbitration agreements and non-disparagement clauses that undermine their ability to report bad behavior or share information about salaries and benefits. Arbitration clauses in employee contracts establish that disputes in cases of harassment must be settled through private arbitration rather than litigation. Arbitration is considered to be more favorable to employers because the process is shielded from public scrutiny and often includes confidentiality and nondisclosure agreements. Non-disparagement clauses prevent individuals from taking any action that might negatively affect an organization, its reputation, products, services, management and employees.

In tech, non-disparagement clauses were designed to prevent employees from leaking trade secrets but often these clauses legally bind individuals not to file public complaints nor speak to the press about inappropriate behavior or sexual harassment. Adria Richards was fired from her job at startup SendGrid after she tweeted about another developer allegedly making sexual jokes during a conference. Reflecting on that incident, one of the interviewees told me: "Gender discrimination and sexual harassment thrived in Silicon Valley hostile macho culture for years and nothing happened. It was public shaming of offenders and bystanders that started to shake things a bit." These arbitration and non-disparagement clauses are a worrisome trend both because they are becoming the norm adopted by big tech companies' codes of conduct. Large companies set the cultural standard for smaller companies. Indeed, why shouldn't smaller companies apply the same low standards? Competition and advantage seeking set the standard behavior for the whole industry. In tech, we talk a lot about one culture but the reality is that there are many subcultures. There is the top-level expression of culture, employee cultures, management cultures, and so on. Diversity and inclusion need to be a collective action requiring coordination to address gender imbalances in big and small companies at the same time.

Parenthood in Silicon Valley

> *"We paid $1,300 for two days of daycare. Yes, we had to put our names on a waiting list and I was terrified that it would take up to 6-8 months, the normal waiting time in other daycare centers on campus. But, we were lucky and got a spot in 2 months. I still had to turn down a job offer because of a combination of issues. First, not knowing if we would have a spot at a daycare and also having a potential employer not being flexible. The expectation was that I had to start working full time at 100% but what they really meant was working at 110%. If they hire you full time, of course they expect you to be available from 7:00 AM to 7:00 PM or sometime later."*
>
> —*Maggie R., public health specialist and educator, Palo Alto*

In Silicon Valley, we observe some interesting family patterns and parenthood dynamics. The long work day and the high cost of living are constant source of stress for most. This combination influences, sometimes determines, how family interactions are established or disturbed. First, in most families, women continue to be responsible for the majority of household and family member care work. In part, this is because men are still not willing to help with household chores. Still, in most cases, the decision to impose this burden on the women is the family's pragmatic decision. Men often have income potential and prospects that are superior to their female spouses. Jane is a doula (someone trained to assist women during childbirth and the family after the baby is born) who has been working in Silicon Valley for ten years. She has helped more than 150 families bring children into the world. Jane told me that one of the most common challenges women face is adjusting expectations to real life. "The impact a baby has in the lives of these families is so profound. Often, the moms say that they plan to go back to work after birth but then they change their minds. It is a process to watch how things unfold because the image of ourselves usually includes the job and position we hold. We do not live in the age that women just leave a job to raise a family. And, if you have a well-paying job, it is hard to let go of that." Jane explained that this is only one of the challenges. A concern dear to her heart is the impact of a competitive environment on plans for breastfeeding. "When I ask women about their plans for breastfeeding, they usually answer: 'if I can, I will breastfeed.' This answer shows that, for them, breastfeeding is optional. The American Pediatric Society recommends six months of exclusive breastfeeding and continuing breastfeeding for one year. These are educated women and when it doesn't work, when they are not successful in breastfeeding, they feel guilty and ashamed." Jane is passionate about her advocacy for breastfeeding. "We need to be more honest about the messaging on breastfeeding. Sometimes, women who wanted to breastfeed don't know that it is hard work and requires a lot of emotional strength and perseverance."

Married to it

In Silicon Valley, men are usually employed in tech companies with high salaries while women tend to hold low paying jobs. Sometimes, however, salary differences within couples result simply because most men are older than their wives and thus further along in their careers. Foreign workers recipients of H1B visas, recruited by third parties are predominantly male. Their spouses come to the U.S. as recipients of H-4 visas that do not allow them to work.

> "My husband came for a PhD program here at Stanford. I came as his spouse. I don't understand why I have to be a stay-home wife. We live in a very expensive region. It is hard to get by on only one person's income. In France, I was an independent woman. I had my career, my money. I didn't need to be supported by anyone. But here, when they ask me what I do, I have to say that I don't work because I am not allowed to work. I take photography, I do hula hooping, volunteer work but I'm always stressed. I am a teacher specialized in education for children with special needs. I speak several languages but they don't acknowledge my skills. I feel like I'm forced to live in the 1930s."
>
> —Mabel N., Menlo Park

In addition, government policies also play a role in decisions made by men and women about how to combine parenthood and work. The U.S. lags behind other developed nations with regards to maternity leave, paid leave, paid sick time, and access to childcare. The U.S. is among the least supportive countries in terms of unemployment benefits including job search assistance and training.[42] In addition, tax treatment of married couples raises the tax rate for secondary earners or the spouse with lower earnings. Because secondary earners are usually women, the current tax system in effect contributes to imbalances that discourage women's participation in the workforce.[43]

> *"After the birth of our third child, I started working from home. I started working 10 hours a week that turned out to be increasing hours. I have specialized knowledge and a huge career. If I give up or take a break, it will be hard to go back. Also, because I've been doing this for some time, it is hard for them to replace me. If I stop, they would need to go to the market and find a full time person and my position will no longer exist. I'd like not to have to check email 24/7 but tuning out is not an option. My husband and I talk about the future every day. I love the idea that we could "cash out" and move somewhere where we have a home and not have a mortgage. I don't have time to sleep. I hire a part-time nanny for 10 hours a week but I have 30 hour commitments. I was a college athlete. Now, I'm horribly out of shape. I would work out at least one hour in the morning but I feel that I physically can't."*
>
> *—Heather E., Menlo Park*

The equation determining labor force participation between married couples is even more unbalanced after the birth of a child. Childcare costs are prohibitive for many families in the region. As of January 2018, a daycare center near Stanford charged $2,100 per month for full time—5 days a week-care and has a wait list of 6-8 months. An experienced babysitter in Palo Alto does not charge less than $18 per hour. "At the end of the day, whoever is making the most money is the center of family decisions and we accommodate to their needs," a new mom told me.

It seems that only women need to balance work and personal life. Men stick to their work life; families adapt their lives around them. Even when fathers are at home, there is no connection with family since expectations are for them to work very, very long hours. Families also have to make accommodations to work schedules that include a lot of travel where husbands are gone out of town for weeks at time, for work. Some of the mothers interviewed described how their families had to adapt to travel schedules by changing children's sleeping times so that they could facetime or skype to talk with their fathers. Often, fathers come home after work tired and need to sleep immediately because they have important meetings later. Mothers, on the other hand, are usually sleep deprived but feel it necessary to stay on top of their children's education and activities. They also feel the need to remain connected to the world and relevant to society. In our society, being a woman usually means living with the constant feeling, even fear, that whatever you are doing, you should also be doing something else, as well. Women continue at this unsustainable pace for a while until they finally pull the plug sometimes withdrawing from the labor market altogether.

> "I am very aware of communicating and sharing chores. We are both working full time but it is interesting how he perceives himself as contributing more in doing house chores than I perceive him contributing. Both of us are at our maximum and it is not enough. I think there is a lot of work in the house to be done and administered. We are doing our best and it seems that we are always unorganized and messy. If I could pay for a nanny and a number of things that I can't afford, life would be so much easier."
>
> —Madeline L., San Francisco

Having no family together time contradicts the image of a perfect family and reinforces a child-centric life for both working and non-working women. For Silicon Valley mothers, in particular, nothing is more important than their children. Children are their number one priority and to whom they must devote themselves completely above anyone and anything else. As parents, they themselves are high achievers and expect nothing less from their children. They organize complex and elaborate schedules of extra-curricular activities. Geographic distances and the lack of a robust public transportation system, translate into many hours of commute time. Mothers generally do the driving. Carpooling among families is common but provides only partial assistance to families and then only among those with similarities in background, interests, and socio-economic status.

> *"The environment for kids is very hard here. The expectations are so high. Even if you choose not to be part of the structured activities, you will not have anyone to play with because everyone else is taking structured activities. I used to spend 32 hours per week driving my kids to and from school and after-school activities. This is a full time job. My daughter was doing competitive dance 5 to 6 days per week. My son was in soccer. They also had music lessons, math tutoring... People don't talk about the mental capacity and energy that goes into managing all these activities, school projects, doctor appointments, school concerts. Parents are responsible for their children's success and this has an impact on families. Because children are so busy and their job is to be good students, do their homework, take the SATs and College Prep SAT, and AP exams, no one expects them to help around the house. I didn't want them to worry about that. It was all on me. I have often felt I have not been able to work out and take care of myself as I'd like to. My husband would say that that is my choice but when you are managing so much, something has to give."*
>
> —*Anna D., mechanical engineer, Redwood City*

In my interviews, some of the women, who were also mothers who left the workforce to care for their children, elaborated on their choice to stay out of the workforce. One particular compelling argument repeated almost like a chorus: children need parents who are present and supportive at all times of their lives. Maternity leave is very important even if babies and toddlers will likely not remember the time spent with them. Later, children in their middle school and teenagers during their high school years undergo important transitions that these mothers want to be a part of. These women cherish the relationship they have with their children and even more the lasting memories they can make together.

> *"My sister gave me some advice that was the best. She said, kids need you more when they are in middle school and high school. I left my job when my youngest was in 7th grade. It is hard to leave your babies to go to work. In the beginning, it feels wrong but I would not have to worry about other things that come up later such as homework, friendships, substance abuse. I was present for my kids during important times and feel I was part of their lives. Children remember things later in life. They remember me being there to support them when they needed me."*
>
> *—Sandra M., retired product manager,*
> *Menlo Park*

Let's Talk About Money: The VC and Startup Worlds

"I think Silicon Valley has its own culture. People here work incredible long hours. My clients work ridiculous hours and I end up working like crazy. I see clients on Saturdays and sometimes on Sundays. I think it is because I am extremely driven and do not always balance things very well. When you start your own business, you tend to take all the work that comes to you. You say 'yes' to everything. Sometimes, I feel I could say no but I don't like to disappoint and end up saying 'yes'. It is hard to take vacation if you are a small business owner. But, isn't it like this everywhere?"

—*Carla M., San Mateo*

SILICON VALLEY HAS DEVELOPED largely as a result of three key elements: (1) progressive legislation on immigration that allows for the provision of services from farm work to elderly care while enabling tech companies to recruit the best talent from anywhere in the world; (2) Stanford University, generating the brain power, promoting research and inspiring the local culture; and (3) generous financial support of the U.S. government, especially the U.S. Department of Defense and, more recently, through venture capital firms. We have discussed the first two key elements in previous chapters. Now, let's talk about money.

Worldwide, government funding and venture capital are important in supporting innovation because they are allowed to take risks where banks are not. This way, government funding and venture capital stimulate the economy resulting in a multiplier effect that creates value for society as a whole. Throughout the country, government financing of military science and military industrial research was intensified during both World Wars and in the context of the Cold War. In the Bay Area, government funding focused on the military. During World War II, between 1941 and 1945, the U.S. Government invested an estimated $70 billion in defense and war-related industry in California.[1] Right from the start, government investment was related to the military science of radar technology, the atomic bomb, submarines, aircraft and digital computers. Uranium research and the Manhattan project first started at Berkley's Radiation Laboratory. In the East Coast, government funding fostered collaborative knowledge production with academics (professors and researchers) at MIT and Harvard University. In Silicon Valley, mainly because corporations and labs were spread out across a relatively large area with little inter-company communication, funding fostered a culture of intense competition and secrecy.[2] As government spending was gradually reduced, private venture capital firms pushed this regional competitive dynamic to expand by offering seed capital to a select group of businesses. In the late 1990s, with the dot-com boom characterized by a rapid rise in equity markets of internet-based companies, many of the VC firms in the region made a killing. Of course, government spending and VC firms are only as successful as the startups and entrepreneurs they support. Even in the 1970s, while the rest of the country struggled with the oil shock crisis, President Ronald Regan praised Silicon Valley's "jog creation machine" and called its entrepreneurs the "pioneers of tomorrow."[3] It was an effective message that validated competition at a personal level and reinforced the myth of meritocracy. This way, financially and symbolically, government favoritism for Silicon Valley's tech industry helped propel the idea of entrepreneurs as heroes and of startups as the engine of job growth in the U.S.

As heroes, Silicon Valley entrepreneurs are recognized and admired for their courage and achievements even if they fail. In the Valley, failure is not viewed as catastrophic. If you fail, you learn and accumulate experience. Failure is seen as an inevitable part of growth and success. Many successful founders have a failed company in their portfolio. What matters is the vision, the passion that drives entrepreneurs and their startups. However, some entrepreneurs are more idealized than others, and some startups are able to raise more funds than others. Over the years, something might have gotten lost. At one point, new startup seemed to pursue technology attempting to solve every social ill. Today, we live in a bubbly era of numerous startups that propose innocuous but profitable uses of technology. The drive to transform society through technological innovation has withered.

There are many studies that support the popular perception that small businesses are important job generators in an economy. According to the Small Businesses Administration (SBA), small businesses, consistently produce more innovations and create more jobs than Fortune 500 companies throughout the full business cycle.[4] But, are the claims we make about small businesses also valid for startups? Small businesses in the U.S. are defined as firms with fewer than 500 employees that generate less than $7 million in sales. Startups in the Valley, however, have many definitions that vary from a "state of mind" to "the pulse of the future". In practical terms, a startup in the Valley is a company that has recently begun its business (usually with five or less years of operation) and which has an exponential potential for growth. Certainly, the idea of a startup is connected to innovation and tech but startups are not necessarily limited to tech innovation. In fact, most businesses in the area are nicknamed startup. Lucy a successful real estate agent in the region jokes: "Today even real estate agencies call themselves startups! They bring cheese and wine to open houses and say that they are innovating!"

If you consider startups to be general businesses with less than five years of operation, then women thrive in the startup world. In 2012, California had the highest absolute number of women-owned firms (over 365 thousand firms) in the U.S.[5] Rhode Island and New York had the highest percentage of women-owned businesses relative to men-owned and equally-owned business with 51.5% and 51.3% respectively. From 1997 to 2015, firms started by non-minority women, African American women, and by Latinas grew 40%, 322% and 224% respectively.[6] Compared to men-owned and equally-owned businesses, women-owned companies dominate the fields of health care and social assistance (88.8%), educational services (58.7%), administrative support, waste management and remediation services (58.7%).[7] Driving up and down El Camino Real, the main road between Highways 280 and 101 that goes through all the major cities in Silicon Valley, one finds women-owned businesses that vary from wellness and fitness centers, to restaurants and software development companies.[8] As one female entrepreneur told me: "Women are competitive not by nature but by choice and need. They must learn to become business savvy to succeed."

Startups and small businesses are also an attractive employment alternative for men and women because they help break the cycle of needing experience to get a job and needing a job to gain experience. A startup or non-profit may provide work in a desired area helping women gain a foothold in dream positions or transition from one industry to another. While, in general, big tech companies in Silicon Valley require at least 10 years of experience for a managerial position, startups usually are willing to gamble. As one interviewee described the view of startups, "Hey, take a chance on us and if we are successful, we will reward you with ownership that will make you rich." This is the stuff of dreams. In most startups, everyone has to work, multitask and do everything to keep operations afloat and a common vision alive. However, tasks often get distributed according to traditional gender roles. Somehow, even in tech startups women end up being responsible for cleaning the dishes and tidying up. More broadly, in startups, women still confront the same issues of gender discrimination, pay inequality and subtle status intimidation. Some of the women reported that co-working spaces are not always safe environments for women. "There is a party culture where young men go to places like a kink room or an adult virtual reality room. "The good thing is that we can talk about this, which can lead to change," said a young female entrepreneur. However, she might have expressed her overly optimistic view of the startup world. There seems to be an existential contradiction between the startups' proclaimed mission of solving the world's problems and their inability to address one of the world's oldest problems: sexism. For instance, many startups don't usually have a clear set of internal rules much less a robust human resources department. Thus, women do not have anyone they can resort to in case of inappropriate behavior. There is no one to file, much less to investigate complaints. In a survey on sexism and harassment, respondents said sexual harassment went unaddressed because there was no human resource or higher authority to report to.[9] When present, human resources are perceived as means for the company to protect itself from lawsuits and rather than to protect employees from abuse.

Startups are notorious for overlooking traditional organizational structures including human resources. Rules of engagement are not necessarily written down. Instead, startups focus on raising cash, being fast, making work "fun", and providing employees with benefits, perks and, yes, ping-pong tables. Fun and perks are important not only because startups compete with big tech companies for talent but also because the turnover in the sector is very high. In the local culture, people pride themselves as being driven and by the ability to quit their jobs and start something new. Everything is fast and ever changing in Silicon Valley. The combination of all these elements has created a culture of permissiveness when it comes to harassment and discrimination.

If we define startups as companies with fewer than five years of operation that are able to raise VC money then, Silicon Valley startups are predominantly male. The distribution of financing is heavily influenced by stereotyping against women. In 2016, women-led companies made up 4.94% of all VC deals. Between 2010 and 2015, only 12% of venture rounds and 10% of venture dollars globally went to startups with at least one woman founder.[10]

While male-founded startups received $58.2 billion in 2016, women-founded startups received only $1.46 billion.[11] That is, men are 40 times more likely than women to receive VC funding.

Networking

Venture capital funds are distributed in rounds depending on the development stage of the business, the investors involved, and the purpose and allocation of requested funds. Rounds begin with "seed capital" to develop a product followed by funding to optimize the product phases A, develop and expand market reach in phase B, and perfect and scale up fast and wide in phase C. Initial decisions about funding are based on market research that maps out potential users or consumers for a given product to be developed. When uncertainty is high regarding a new product or market potential, assessment of the entrepreneur's potential becomes central in the VC's decision. Meritocracy turns into a fairy tale.

Many would agree that raising funds has very little to do with personal merits and a lot to do with your social networks and referrals. In Silicon Valley, value is placed on social networks and personal relations. In the local culture, networking is critical. In Silicon Valley, networking is an "art." It can determine if you get hired, your career success, and if you are a tech venture, your likelihood of raising investment. A young Stanford graduate co-founder and executive director of a tech startup put it bluntly: "I never had to apply for a job in a traditional way. I got all my jobs though networks." Techies actively network in many ways. The most straight forward approach is to showcase and share your expertise with colleagues that might benefit from it. To succeed here you need an attitude of self-promotion, a readiness to always present your work in the grandest way possible. One woman complained about social life in San Francisco by explaining that "You can't go out to a party and meet new people without being pitched a new business idea." It is also very common for professionals to work as brokers connecting one community to another in and out of tech. It is perfectly acceptable to seek out meetings with people that excel in their fields even though you have never met them. People are usually available to meet and talk to perfect strangers provided they see value in the interaction or if they are properly introduced by a member of their networks. To some, networking can feel laborious and disingenuous. Still, most interviewed agreed that exclusion from a network either voluntarily or involuntarily such as by taking some time off can be social (and professional) suicide.

The intensity by which one's reputation and potential needs to be validated by a network can put women and people of color in disadvantaged positions. First, networking validates criteria based on personal favoritism. In addition, the networking process relies on a self-referential framework in which people in power tend to favor those that look and act like them. White males will refer and endorse other white men. Not only are VCs predominantly white and male, traditionally, women and people of color lack access to formal or informal networks. For women and people of color, this presents two challenges: first, engaging the right social networks and then, getting past the white male gatekeepers. An African American woman explained: "Silicon Valley is a whole ecosystem, tech, VCs, education, etc. The whole set of values and behaviors and many are related to aggression and masculinity like the idea that it is easier to ask for forgiveness than for permission. There is also a high value placed on engineering and logic devaluating of other disciplines. It is all about who you know, what school you go to, what shoes you wear, and social markers that if you are in you recognize and if you are not in, you don't know."

Even when networking is supposed to take place during freewheeling parties, women attendees are not included in similar terms as white men. For instance, during some of these networking parties women are encouraged to become intimate with other guests. Women who attend those gatherings sometimes may be aggressively pursued and sexually harassed by colleagues. Those who do not attend might miss out on important business deals.[12] As a woman, you are dammed if you do and dammed if you don't.

In the 1980s, startup activity benefited immensely from moonlighting,[13] the practice of working on an entrepreneurial project while being employed by another company and from women who had stable manufacturing jobs. Women in manufacturing were able to send their children to college and support their husbands while they adventured in entrepreneurial tech projects. Most people are risk averse. If you live from pay check to pay check, it might never cross your mind to open a business, or to develop a startup. Women in manufacturing jobs provided the safety net for men to take risks. The average age in a startup then was higher because knowledge and some experience in the industry/manufacturing was a de facto requirement. In the 1990s, that changed. First, most of the manufacturing jobs were gone and women were displaced from the labor market in the region. The Dot-com era, roughly from 1995 to 2001, lowered the capital requirement for startups and the age of those involved. As a result, young men attracted to the business started to flock and dominate the tech industry in Silicon Valley while women found themselves trying to catch up to a moving target. This high concentration of young men in the industry meant that the older male "control" authority of unacceptable behavior was lost. It was the ascension of the bro-culture.

The VC world also changed around the same time. In the beginning VCs were industry insiders. They were people with operating experience. Now, VCs are often outsiders, professional financiers that offer money but not much knowledge or expertise. In addition, today most of the VC investment goes exclusively to biotech and software companies. These transformations that altered the nature of startups and VC firms turned Silicon Valley into a strange ecosystem in which entrepreneurs and venture capitalists validate one another based on returns and hardly ever question the means used to get results. Critics call this an echo-chamber moved by greed and hyper-growth. There are very few disclosure requirements, almost no transparency or any system for monitoring and investigating accusations of improper behavior. Investors and board members are focused on a company's growth and return. Workplace problems such as gender discrimination and harassment are rarely, if ever, assessed by investors.

In addition, VC firms struggle with their own accusations of gender biases, discrimination and harassment. If it weren't difficult enough for women to get startup funding due to men's failure to understand products that focus on women's needs,[14] women entrepreneurs face systematic discrimination. The problem with VC discrimination is not exclusive to Silicon Valley. Wall-Street and Madison Avenue have also been male-dominated fields with similar behavior. Cases from New York, London, Berlin, and São Paulo support the idea that gender discrimination knows no regional boundaries. Yet, one woman very familiar with VC firms described the VC world in Silicon Valley as the "bro culture on steroids." She told me: "They are a small and secretive group that holds a lot of power and money." A study that recorded VCs conversations and analyzed how the language they use to refer to female founders differs from the language used for male founders revealed that money may not be invested in businesses with the highest potential. According to that study, men were usually characterized as having more entrepreneurial potential than women thus affecting who got funding and who didn't. Common attributes used to describe an average male entrepreneur were "young and promising," "experienced and knowledgeable", and "very competent innovator and already with money to play with" while women entrepreneurs were described as "young, but inexperienced," "experienced but worried," and "good-looking and careless with money."[15]

Sometimes, VC firms claim that to become a general partner, one must have founded or led a significant tech company as CEO. This rule was intrinsically biased against women but it was not the only barrier to the promotion of women as general partners in VC firms. In addition, female founders are sometimes subject to sexual harassment and male predatory behavior. Ellen Pao's example of speaking out against discrimination and inappropriate behavior in a prestigious venture capital firm, Kleiner Perkins Caufield & Byers, paved the way for other women in the region. Early in 2017, seven women spoke out about unwanted and inappropriate advances made by Binary Capital co-founder, Justin Caldbeck.[16] After investors in the fund threatened to pull out, Caldbeck resigned. More than two dozen women in Silicon Valley's tech startups have told *The New York Times* about being sexually harassed in the industry.[17] "I'm a creep. I'm sorry" was the title of an apology by Dave McClure, general partner at a seed investment group 500 Startups, after sexual harassment complaints by a female founder.[18] McClure casually admitted making inappropriate advances towards multiple women in work-related situations in a blog post that was the ultimate expression of just how much men of his position believe that it is easier to ask for forgiveness than to ask for permission.

For many women, regret and apologies come too late. Women that suffer sexual advances not only have less chance of successfully raising funds but may also suffer from depression. Some startup entrepreneurs may give up the whole idea of venture capital opting instead to "bootstrap" using personal finances, the new company's revenue, or may try to survive by relying on funds raised among friends and family relatives. A woman I'll call Maggie, after telling me about her experience and perspective explained that "the feeling that there is something that keeps you from doing what you are capable of is very frustrating." Then, she added: "I could feel all my frustration turning into rage. It was a tipping point. So I decided not to take any equity from outside investors. That was one of the best decisions I ever made."

In 2017, California legislator, Sen. Hannah-Beth Jackson introduced a new bill (Senate Bill 224) aimed at establishing express sanctions for investors who harass founders.[19] The bill updates a section of the Unruh Civil Rights Act that prohibits sexual harassment between people who have a business relationship but don't work for the same company. The new law tries to clarify a traditional grey area in the legislation through which founders were not covered because they were not considered employees. This bill is a step forward. Legislation must be revised to respond to changing circumstances, protect women effectively, and periodically updated.

Part of the problem that leads to harassment is the power differential between men and women in leadership roles. Only 7% of the partners in the top 100 venture firms are women.[20] To correct this imbalance, in the past few years, women VCs have been opening their own funds like the Female Founders Fund and female-friendly work spaces, incubators and accelerators like Pinkubator and Reboot Accel. One more groundbreaking female VCs of our times are Theresia Gouw and Jennifer Fonstad of Aspect Ventures, Elizabeth Yin at the Hustle Fund, Cynthia Ringo of DBL Investors, Kristen Green at Forerunner Ventures, Anu Duggal of Female Starters Fund, and Susan Lyne of BBG Ventures. Angel investor groups such as Astia Angels and Golden Seeds also give women more options for funding their startups. With the new women's funds help working to level the playing field by investing in women-funded businesses, we may see an increase in the representation of women in the startup world. Because female-founded tech startups are more likely to hire more women[21] and create more female-friendly products, bro-culture eventually will face "wo-culture".

The gender gap in funding will not be completely solved simply because there are more women VCs. Traditional VC firms still control larger funds and are led mainly by white males. In those firms, despite efforts to diversify, women take a long time to make partners and top women VCs rarely see a woman replace them. In addition, women who evaluate startups can display the same biases in their evaluation favoring male entrepreneurs over female founders.[22] There are also women who are complicit with the patriarchal system at work. For example, some women say that women should stop whining about their "bad-experiences". Complicity may also be expressed when a problem is ignored. The motto here is: "If I can do it, so can you."

"My friend recruited me to work at a VC firm. It was super competitive but with a much better pay. I could pay off school loans. It was hard to get the job and they told me how hard it was when they gave me the process feedback. But, working for them was the worst 10 months of my life. It was not the men. It was the women. I didn't understand why it was so difficult. What was supposed to be great turned out to be a miserable experience. It was a typical mean girl environment, so toxic, back stabbing. So, I quit the job. It was horrible. I took some time off and traveled before starting my new job. This experience opened my eyes to a lot of things."

—Sarah K., Palo Alto

There have also been some reports of possible backlash from male VCs. Men threatened not to work with women to avoid risks such as reputational damage or expensive legal proceedings. Sheryl Sandberg, Facebook COO, noted angry male reactions to the burst of sexual allegations. She wrote in a post that she had heard comments such as "this is why you shouldn't hire women."[23] In later presentations, Sandberg has noted that the #MeToo movement has left half of male managers "afraid" of holding dinner or one-on-one meetings with female employees.[24] It is not productive to speculate about all the possible collateral damage that male VCs might inflict to the cause of gender diversity and inclusion nor invest our energy in initiatives that cut out men entirely. Sandberg's anecdotal warnings describe male behavior that is either ignorant of the #MeToo movement or made in bad faith. Polarization is not the answer. If men are afraid because of ignorance, then they need to be educated. Despite the recent wave of revelations of sexual harassment, there are many cases that have not been brought to light. The #MeToo is only the beginning of a conversation and a call for change. If men are "afraid" because of bad faith, they need to be called out.

There is no question that men must be part of the debate on gender inclusion. Patriarchy can be limiting for boys and men as it is for girls and women. Perhaps precisely because they are in positions of power, men must be part of the solution as allies and advocates. Some already are. Lewis Gersh, CEO for PebblePost, has been a supporter of diversity efforts and when serving as a local VC managed a portfolio comprised of 40% female and/or minority founders. LinkedIn Founder Reid Hoffman called other VCs to sign a Decency Pledge.[25] For years, men have provided mentorship and sponsorship that have helped women get to where we are. We should be able to count on men to reach even further. By supporting women-and minority-owned startups and demonstrating genuine commitment to diversity and inclusion, VCs can influence the Silicon Valley community and leave a legacy of promoting innovation and justice.

People Like Us: Can Solidarity and Giving Back Save Silicon Valley?

ONCE, THE LAND WHERE Silicon Valley is located, along the margins of the San Francisco Bay, was part of the Ohlone territory. The Ohlones barely survived contact with missionaries and Spanish. Of the few cultural Ohlone expressions that survived is a refrain from a hunting song: "Dancing on the brink of the world." The refrain references a way of life in a bountiful region but also carries a sense of warning.

Today, there is a certain glamour in living to Silicon Valley. It is a scenic location with communities spreading at the base of foothills alongside rivers, creeks and streams. When approaching the region by plane, one of the tallest buildings is the iconic Spanish inspire Hoover Tower at Stanford. The adjacent hills are covered with beautiful vegetation that include the giant Redwood trees, California oak and, at the right time, delicate wildflowers and colorful California poppy. If you go up to the summit of the nearby hills, you get spectacular views of the San Francisco Bay on the side of the Valley and the Pacific Ocean on the other. It is beautiful. The temperate climate is pleasant for the vegetation in general and ideal for almost all kinds of fruit. It is common to see fruit trees, oranges, lemons, persimmons, pomegranate, and many more in front of houses and in and around the Stanford campus. Although Silicon Valley cities are the largest employers in the region, there is a suburban feel, with single-family homes and gardens rather than high-rise buildings across the landscape.

Part of the glamour of living in Silicon Valley also comes from the feeling that this is the center of the universe for innovation and technology. This is the place you have to be because at any instant, in a startup operating out of a garage somewhere, someone is developing the next big idea that will change our future. However, in the brink of the world, people are starting to realize that the prestige of living in Silicon Valley comes at a very high cost. First, it is unlikely that the next transformative idea will come out of a garage startup run by a nobody; and if it does, Google or Facebook will buy it before we even hear about it. In practice, big tech companies control the flow of information and innovation pathways. They move forward quickly with little regard for the consequences of their actions on people, institutions and even political systems.

> *"When I first moved here, I didn't feel welcome. I thought the infrastructure was really expensive and outdated. The area grew so rapidly and the tech companies provide everything for their workers that there is no need to update things like roads, public spaces, restaurants. I was really not impressed. Some things are advanced like the grocery delivery service but in general I thought that once people settled here, they didn't worry about the community any more. They just took things for granted."*
>
> —*Nadia T., educator, Mountain View*

The tech giants have expanded their missions, their global reach but also physically. In the next years, Google plans an 18.6 acre expansion for its Mountain View campus[1] as well as in San Jose and Sunnyvale to accommodate over 31,000 new employees.[2] Apple Park is a 175-acre campus expansion in Cupertino.[3] In 2015, Facebook opened its 430,000 square-foot megaplex in Menlo Park. Expansion is the exclusive prerogative of the big tech companies. Stanford University plans an expansion of 2.3 million square feet of new academic buildings and about 3,150 new housing units to accommodate another 9,000 students, faculty and staff branching out from Palo Alto to Redwood City.[4] Their continuous expansion of academic and work campuses has created a dramatic housing crisis in Silicon Valley, where the median sale prices for a home is over $1 million. The cost of living is among the highest in the country with rents for rustic accommodations at around $3,000 per month.[5]

> *"Our school lost 40 teachers last year. If you want to be a social worker, a teacher, a police officer, you can't afford to live here. People are pragmatic about family decisions. If you can't earn a living to be here, you have to move out. It messes up your mind."*
>
> —*Emily C. Menlo Park*

Silicon Valley residents often juggle two or three mortgage loans to afford a house in the region. "People don't realize how demanding it is to live in Silicon Valley. People see the glamour but it is definitely an extremely hard life. It is not for everybody. It is for a niche of people that decide that this is what they want for their lives and for their future," explained a freelancer journalist. Increasingly, people are coming to the realization that something is wrong in paradise. Tech innovations are source of pride. Yet a growing number of people now blame the tech industry for a toxic and damaging culture of gentrification and lack of community engagement. Protesters have picketed tech shuttle buses and displayed signs urging "techies go home."[6]

Scratch the calm surface and appearance and you will find that most families struggle to survive here. In 2010, one out of every three households (33.5%) in Santa Clara County could not afford a basic standard of living, a considerable increase since 2000 when 24.1% of households could not afford that minimum standard of living.[7] In 2015, the Silicon Valley Institute for Regional Studies revealed that three in ten Silicon Valley residents don't earn enough to support themselves.[8] Among those are most of tech's "invisible workers," security officers, retail clerks, plumbers, janitors, drivers, cooks and landscapers.

"You try to sell things on craigslist, create a blog, become a yoga instructor, a dog-walker, do whatever it takes to survive and stay here," a woman who worked in a local non-profit told me. Those unable to earn enough to live here are forced out. Big tech companies' constant and increasing need for personnel brings thousands of tech workers to San Francisco and Silicon Valley. This has enticed real estate speculators hoping to cash in on fast tech money. As a result, long-time local residents, poorer, seniors, Hispanics and African-Americans are being displaced from their homes. It is hard to find cashiers to work in grocery stores or waiters to work in restaurants because the workers cannot afford to live or even commute into the region.[9] Already, teachers, firemen and police officers serving the cities in Silicon Valley face long daily commutes. Public transportation options in the Valley are limited intensifying traffic. The commute is slow and expensive. According to the Metropolitan Transportation Commission (MTC), since 2010, traffic congestion in the Bay Area has increased 80%. The average driver in 2016 spent about 3.5 minutes per commute traveling less than 35mph, a 9 percent increase from 2015.[10]

Many of those who can't afford to buy or rent live in vehicles parked on side streets or hidden parking lots. Still, these residents are visible to all who care to see on El Camino Real between Stanford University and the upscale Palo Alto Town and Country Mall. At times, these families will move to emergency shelters and transitional housing but temporary housing is also scarce. One consequence of the housing crisis is the surge in the number of homeless people that spread from San Francisco throughout Silicon Valley. The number of homeless in Mountain View nearly doubled from 139 in 2013, to 276 in 217 and rose again in 2017 to 416 people.[11] Men, women and children will stand near traffic lights holding cardboards to express their plea: "Help."

> *"Housing prices are very high here. I have three daughters. They all live in our house and rent from us. My youngest is 36. She is a nurse. My oldest is in high tech. She works in three jobs but it is part of her personality. It is very difficult for them to move out. Personally, I'm thinking about moving to Sacramento. There is an exodus from Silicon Valley into the Sacramento area. The ones who leave are mainly young families and people who have retired. Maybe this move will open up some availability for the new comers."*
>
> *—Lisa D. Hotel manager, Palo Alto*

The housing crisis and economic instability affect women in particular ways. For example, house prices can influence a family's decision to have a baby. Estimates indicate that a $10,000 increase in house value also increases the fertility rate in 5% for home owners and decreases it by 2.4% among non-owners. [12] Another impact of the housing crisis that affects women severely is domestic violence. In general, women and children, survivors of domestic violence are often discriminated against, denied access to, and even evicted from housing. [13] Domestic violence is among the leading causes of homelessness for women and children. In California, a test conducted by the Equal Rights Center found that 65% of those seeking housing on behalf of domestic violence survivors were denied housing or offered less advantageous terms in housing contracts.[14] In addition, because women tend to be in low-income industries, low-wage and often in informal jobs, where sexual harassment protections are not fully in place, it is harder to confront mistreatment and not uncommon for abuse, discrimination and harassment to go under the radar. In Silicon Valley, with rents as high as they are the pressure to endure domestic violence and other forms of abuse is much greater.

There is also a link between the housing crisis and increased racial segregation in the region as the housing crisis disproportionately affects Latinos and African-Americans. Perhaps these contrasts are more evident in the city of East Palo Alto. Right in the heart of the most prosperous region in the world, East Palo Alto happens to be surrounded by Google and NASA Research Center in Mountain View, Facebook in Menlo Park, Stanford University and the City of San Francisco. Despite the enormous wealth nearby, in 2016, 16.6% of East Palo Alto residents lived below the poverty line and the average yearly income per person was just $20,336.[15] By contrast to its neighboring white-majority towns, 64.5% of East Palo Alto's population is Hispanic or Latino, 16.7% is Black or African American, 3.8% Asian.[16] More than one-third of East Palo Alto students are homeless, sharing homes with other families because their parents can't afford their own home, or living in RVs and shelters.[17] The city is fighting gentrification by instituting strict rent control laws and designating areas for low-income housing but residents feel it is not nearly enough. As one Latina woman I interviewed put it: "Tech is like Pac Man eating everything and everyone around it."

The public school system is also a good indicator that something is not working well in Silicon Valley. State budget cuts have generated a school system that is under-resourced and ranks among the last states in student-to-teacher ratios and school-nurse-per-student ratios. Per-student spending in Silicon Valley's schools has been declining for years and getting more unequal with the wealthiest school district in the region spending nearly $6,000 more per student than the poorest.[18] This stark contrast clashes with the legacy that Stanford co-founders wished to create, one that would employ their wealth to help "other people's" children.[19] Yet, Stanford gives very little back to the public schools in the area, in contrast with contributions made by Harvard and MIT to the city of Cambridge, Massachusetts and its schools. Stanford's example is followed by the big tech companies in the region. Combining the effects of the housing crisis and the lack of funding, some schools in the region are becoming rapidly more segregated. A school administrator at Palo Alto Unified School District told me that in the 2018 graduating class of 600 students at Palo Alto High School, there were only six Black students.

High income concentration has been linked to systems that perpetuate social inequality also producing race and gender discrimination. Many studies show that wealthier individuals tend to be both less ethical and less generous than others exhibiting a reduced sense of empathy and connectedness.[20] This can be observed in attitudes that undermine the efforts to include women in the tech industry. First, in general, there seems to be a disconnect between reality and people's perceptions about diversity and inclusion in their companies. Men usually think that their companies are more inclusive than they are. For example, despite the overwhelming evidence of biased attitudes towards women and minorities, a 2017 survey 1,400 tech workers on the state of diversity revealed that 94% of respondents give their industry, their companies and their teams a passing grade on diversity.[21] Second, there is a general misunderstanding about what diversity is and what progress looks like. Tech workers often believe their companies are making a considerable effort towards inclusion but cannot articulate what those efforts are. More frequently, they believe that their industry rewards merits above everything else. This is a problem because the discourse of meritocracy is often used to justify discrimination. According to a recent study, the belief in meritocracy makes people more biased in hiring, promoting and rewarding workers.[22] The researchers in the study called it the *paradox of meritocracy*, that is, when organizations explicitly present themselves as meritocratic, individuals in managerial positions favor men over equally performing women.[23] Third, it is true that most major tech companies in Silicon Valley have diversity programs. Yet, most diversity goals are vague and broadly defined. Women feel that men don't understand that offering generous benefits for their employees including flexible hours, maternity leave and the possibility for women to freeze their eggs, it is not synonymous with a welcoming environment for women.

Tech companies and people in Silicon Valley must solve these social ills even if acting on their own self-interest. In the 1980s, Mountain View residents advocated for policies of rent control that would protect its low-income residents. Other cities including San Francisco and East Palo Alto have approved provisions on such measures. In 1996, the Silicon Valley Toxics Coalition, as part of the Campaign for Responsible Technology, drafted a set of guidelines for the high-tech industry. The guidelines, known as the Silicon Principles, included requirements and policies for equal standards for sub-contractors and suppliers, civilian oversight of R&D, worker improvement programs, health and safety education programs, work with the local communities, and monitoring as well as toxic use reduction program among to be implemented locally, nationally and internationally.[24] It may be time for an updated edition of the Silicon Valley Principles.

In this regard, many new nonprofit organizations are stepping up and providing services where corporations and governments have failed. The region has also seeing the resurgence of old and new social movements such as Silicon Rising, a coordinated campaign driven by a coalition of labor, faith leaders, community based organizations and workers. There is the Jesse Jackson initiative and plan for diversity in Silicon Valley that aims to promote tech recruiting on black college campuses, as well as establishing tech corporate offices in areas with underemployed populations such as Detroit.[25] These are also some recent examples of mobilization and response. Civil society and social organizations have a role in promoting inclusion and diversity and mitigating the socio-economic and racial inequalities in the region. In these efforts, unsurprisingly, women are the majority doing the work. There is a genuine interest in the community that it is important to give back.

> *"I think this region is very conducive to volunteering. I wanted to give back. I contribute financially but I also volunteer my time. I think being generous with your time is an important thing. I was on the Board of two schools. I want to know what is going on and to help the kids. I want to be involved at the grassroots level. It is a great experience. The schools are very open and reach out to get help. Parent volunteers reduce the workload for teachers. It helps the schools because they don't have enough money and it frees money for other things. It makes a better community and helps attract good teachers."*
>
> *—Carol H., financial consultant, Menlo Park*

Silicon Valley's wealth has been an important source of philanthropy feeding local nonprofits such as schools, community, and service organizations. Though not widely known, the Silicon Valley Community Foundation is the largest community foundation in the world, awarding grants that have totaled more than $4.3 billion in the past decade.[26] The grants are usually for local charities, non-profits, or pressing causes and issues affecting the region. In the 2008-2009 academic year, between Parent-Teacher

Association (PTA) and Partners in Educations (Palo Alto parent-led nonprofit fundraising organization), parents contributed more than $4 million to the Palo Alto Unified School District.[27] In the U.S., San Francisco and Santa Clara County have the largest number of culturally and ethnically focused organizations per 100,000 residents.[28] That is, organizations who identified using the National Taxonomy of Exempt Organizations (NTEE) code A23 (which refers to "cultural and ethnic awareness organizations"), with missions to support ethnic activity in communities.

> *"I grew up here. I went to Palo Alto High School in the 60s. Back then, it was a middle-class college town but everybody's father worked for a famous company. My friend's parents got Nobel Prizes. All this made me realize at an early age how fortunate I was and I wanted to give back. I give back writing checks but also giving my time. People don't get enough time. Kids don't get to spend time with an adult. To mentor a woman, you need to devote time and giving back became part of who I am."*
>
> —Lucia G., writer and educator, Palo Alto

People give back financially and also donate their own time. Highly qualified women are the basis of an intricate and vibrant social infrastructure that sustains life in Silicon Valley. These women include those affected by visa restrictions that prohibit women who come to the area accompanying their spouses from paid employment as well as women who have opted out of the labor force but need an outlet for their skills. These women offer their free labor to school associations, community organizations, faith-based NGOs and more. Some of these organizations have been quite successful. One way to measure the impact of social movements and nonprofit work is the passage of legislation. The Women's Foundation of California has contributed to the passage of 32 new state laws including the Domestic Workers Bill of Rights extending legal labor protections including overtime pay to 100,000 low-wage workers in California, the majority of whom are women.[29] There are also a number of non-profits that operate in similar terms as conventional startups even raising funds from VCs. These so called nonprofit startups aim to apply technology to promote solutions to global problems. One of these organizations, for example, Think of Us provides foster children an online network of mentors, supporters and friends who can help in their education and transition to adulthood.[30] Others are dedicated to developing human-centered applications using Artificial Intelligence (AI) technology.[31] Together, these non-profit organizations and social movements provide valuable contributions to reduce the socio-economic divides in the region created or accentuated by the tech industry. While important, their efforts have not been sufficient to address all the societal needs.

In the age of "hashtag activism", non-profits organizations face the challenge of mobilizing communities to remain engaged and advocate for policies that promote change. Many local philanthropists are interested in funding high-visibility causes. They don't want to fund homeless shelters or food pantries. In addition, despite generous support from individual donors, Silicon Valley may not be a viable nor sustainable option given financial challenges such as facility rent and operational expenses. In recent years, San Francisco and the region have seen the number of nonprofits decline mainly due to the difficulty to match salaries to the high cost of living in the Bay Area. The work of nonprofit organizations is very important but it is not a substitute for social policies that promote inclusive access to technology, greater support to women-owned businesses and startups, as well as concrete measures to mitigate the pervasive effects of tech industries on poverty and inequality in the region.

In Their Own Words

FROM SEPTEMBER 2017 TO March 2018, I conducted in-depth, semi-structured interviews with one hundred women and two dozen men. Most of the women felt more comfortable speaking to me on condition of anonymity. I opted to extend anonymity to all participants. The interviews provided information on personal perceptions of gender issues in Silicon Valley as well as valuable narratives of historical facts and events that took part in the region. I employed a snowball approach to identify interview participants starting with Stanford students, faculty and staff and later reaching out to women power circles such as Latinas in Tech, Brasileiras do Valle and Lean In Circles in Silicon Valley. From the start, my aim was to interview a variety of women from different ethnicities, socio-economic backgrounds, ages, professions and from industries or activities. Participants' breakdown was White (n=44), Latina/o (n=33), Asian American (n=13), African American (n=10). Of the women interviewed, 28 were working in tech, 40 in services including finance, banking and consulting, 22 were students, in academia or educators, 10 were working for non-profit organizations excluding academia or educational services. In this group, 5 were older than 60, 37 were 46 to 60 years of age, 23 were between 36 and 45 years of age and 35 were between 22 and 35 years of age.

The interviews lasted between thirty minutes to two hours. They were conducted in different locations, including the interviewee's worksite, co-working spaces, their homes, at Stanford campus or in coffee shops. On some occasions, interviews were conducted over the phone. The interview included general questions about the respondent's expectations and hopes for the future as well as advice respondents might want to pass on to women facing similar struggles. Interviews were annotated, digitalized and coded for emergent themes. Themes included the importance of education on promoting gender diversity and inclusion in the workforce, reasons for women to leave the workforce, perceptions on leadership and women's contributions to Silicon Valley in particular and society in general. For background information, I researched academic and journalistic accounts that elucidated themes covered in the interviews. To write this book, I also spent 18 months reviewing literature on Silicon Valley, its history and development, Stanford University, main tech industries and venture capital firms. I have included their insight in the analysis of this book.

The advice women provided could be aggregated in 5 main areas: (1) Confidence; (2) Education and opportunities; (3) Leadership; (4) Networking, mentoring and building community; (5) Wellness, flexibility and life-work balance. Below, I organize some of the advice by area.

Areas	In their words
Confidence	"Women need to know how to articulate what they want and what their skills are. You should not minimize or undermine the accomplishment of raising kids, or your volunteer work. Those are important organizational, administrative and life skills." "I never think I can't do it. I might not do it the first time or be the first but I'll be the second or third. If you are not welcomed, you welcome yourself." "I don't have specific advice but whenever someone reaches out, I'm always available and I tell them this is what I have done and this is how I have done it. Never think that because you are a woman you can't make it happen." "Don't be afraid to fail. Every decision is a learning moment." "Build your style on your own qualities. If you build your style based on other people, you are setting yourself up for failure." "Women tend to downplay their work. Watch your language. Don't say: I'm working on a *little* project, on a *little* research. This is self-sabotaging. It is a big project! It's great research!"
Education and opportunities	"Life in the Valley is rough. You have to have clear goals and planning. Then, you'll find that there are options and possibilities everywhere." "To stay relevant, you have to step outside your comfort zone and diversify your areas of knowledge. You have to be continuously learning." "Be willing to learn new things and get beyond your comfort zone. Commit to ongoing learning about everything that is important to your work." "Extension courses are a cost-effective alternative that let you stay informed and continuously learn." "There are a lot of self-learning opportunities out there and you should take advantage of that." "Women need extra education and an extra star in their resume to outshine the guys." "Learn new things always."

Leadership	"Don't worry about being liked. Worry about being respected."
	"Be strategic. Know how to pick your battles and whenever possible, use humor to address difficult issues."
	"You have to persevere, solve problems. Figure out a way to solve problems in your job. That is how you build a reputation."
	"Communication needs to be your number 1 priority. Speak up. Don't let anyone say you can't do it."
	"Women tend to apologize too much. We wait our turn to present our ideas and don't get the praise or recognition we deserve. My suggestion is to be vocal. Don't hesitate to take credit for your contributions."
Networking, mentoring and building community	"Networking is gold. Be good at it. Go to conferences, meet-ups, listen to what people have to say, ask questions and join support groups."
	"Now we recognize sexual violence and harassment but there was a lot of education that went into that. We need that same level of education and commitment to teach men and women to identify instances of sexism and discrimination."
	"Look for networks.
	"Develop your style. Seek out opportunities. Make your own opportunities."
	"To be successful, find a good mentor."
	"Women don't do for other women what they could. We need to protect and promote ourselves."

Wellness, flexibility and life-work balance	"Productivity is overrated. My advice is first, stay true to yourself. Don't try to be someone you are not. It weakens you and creates anxiety. Understand your strengths and weaknesses and know that it is OK to fail."
	"You need to be clear about what you want. If you want to be happy, if you want to make money, if you want to be famous. People don't usually ask what they want to do. It is important to ask yourself what you want and not be afraid to try something new to get what you want."
	"My advice to women is versatility. You'll run into trouble if you are not flexible."
	"I've been in situations that any job is better than none. But you should remember that temp is *temp*. It puts gas in your car and pays the rent. Temp jobs should be temp for the employer and the employee."
	"Things don't follow a natural path and life takes a lot of turns. Opportunities might come and you need to be flexible."
	"When you are stressed, it is hard to think creatively, which ultimately affects your potential so de-stress and take care of yourself."

Acknowledgements

I MUST FIRST EXPRESS my enormous gratitude to the women and men participants in my research for generously sharing their time and offering invaluable insights to someone (me) very few knew in advance. They opened a window not only into their lives but also a world of possibilities. With every interview I felt energized and motivated. As part of a growing movement pushing for a more just and equal society, they have given me hope and made me an optimist. Thank you.

I would not have been able to reach all the wonderful participants if it weren't for the prompt help from a number of women's organizations in Silicon Valley. In particular, I would like to thank the many members from Latinas in Tech, Brasileiras do Vale, the Career Accelerator for Women, Reboot Accel, and the Lean In Circles, Lean In Latinas and Lean In Latinas of San Mateo County, Wish Events and Bay Brazil.

It is a pleasure for me to acknowledge a number of women's rights activist friends, professional colleagues and relatives who inspired me and consistently offered comments and support. Thank you, Pooja Sancheti, Paula Gobbi and Ken Shulman. Thank you to those who have commented on and supported my work along the way: Prameela Bartholomeusz, Lyris Wiedemann, Natasha Caiado, Noam Shemtov, Alison Crossley, Deborah Popowski, Jennifer Lovitt-Riggs, Maria Oliveira, Eunice Rodriguez, Ramya Srinivasan, and Irma Zoepf. A special thank you to Cate Boyd for her patience in assisting me with editing and publishing this book. I also owe my gratitude to Huifen and Kirk Dunn for their openness, for sharing their knowledge of Silicon Valley but above all, for their friendship.

At Stanford, I'd like to thank Professor Francis Fukuyama for his kindness and intellectual stimulation always. I have been fortunate to have been part of a vibrant intellectual community at Stanford. This made possible, even if in brief interactions meet with some of the leaders of our times including Sheryl Sandberg, Larry Page and personal life heroes such as Dolores Huerta and Angela Davis.

Jim and Mara, thank you so much for your patience and confidence in me. Lucky me to have at home two of the most wonderful critics and editors. I couldn't have done it without your love, and remember: I'll always love you.

References

On the Top of the World

1. Zeitgest, Maria J. "From the Gold Rush to Silicon Valley: How Does the Tech Boom Represent the New Western Dream," *KQED*, 9 Dec. 2014. ww2.kqed.org/pop/2014/10/15/from-the-gold-rush-to-silicon-valley-how-does-the-tech-boom-represent-a-new-western-dream/

2. Lewis-Kraus, Gideon. "One Startup's Epic Struggle to Survive the Silicon Valley Gold Rush." *Wired*, Conde Nast, 27 June 2018, www.wired.com/2014/04/no-exit/.

3. Massaro, Rachel and Jennings, Jill Minnick. "Silicon Valley Population Hits 3 Million." 2017 Silicon Valley Index. Joint Venture Institute for Regional Studies, https://jointventure.org/2017-index-news-release.

4. U.S. Department of Housing and Urban Development, "FY 2018 Income Limits Documentation System." *Low-Income Housing Tax Credits*, HUD www.huduser.gov/portal/datasets/il/il2018/select_Geography.odn

5. "What a Performance." *The Economist*. 28 July 2015. www.economist.com/blogs/graphicdetail/2015/07/silicon-valleys-fortunes?fsrc=scn/tw/te/bl/ed/WhatAPErformance

6. Florida, Richard and King, Karen M. "The Geography of Venture Capital Investment by Metro and Zip Code." Martin Prosperity Institute, University of Toronto, 2016.

7. "Silicon Valley Startups." Angel.co, 2018 https://angel.co/silicon-valley

8. According to Wired, in 2014, there were 15,931 self-identified angel investors in Silicon Valley and 6,282 seed or angel funded startups in San Francisco have gone at least one year without raising VC funds. *Wired.* One Startup's Struggle to Survive Silicon Valley's Gold Rush. Gideon Lewis—Kraus, 04/22/14. Available at: https://www.wired.com/2014/04/no-exit/ Retrieved on 11/12/17.

9. The Kaufman Index of Startup Activity from 1997 to 2016 for the United States. Available at: http://www.kauffman.org/microsites/kauffman-index/rankings/national?Report=StartupActivity Retrieved on 11/12/17.

10. Angel.co—Silicon Valley Startups https://angel.co/silicon-valley Retrieved on 11/12/17.

11. U.S. Department of Health and Human Services, Office on Women's Health. "Chronic Fatigue Syndrome." www.womenshealth.gov/a-z-topics/chronic-fatigue-syndrome

12. See for example, Murphy, Kate and Sanchez, Tatiana. "Jerry Brown signs sweeping California immigration bills into law."*Mercury News*, 6 October 2017. www.mercurynews.com/2017/10/05/jerry-brown-signs-california-immigration-bills-into-law/.

13. National Conference of State Legislatures (NCSL). "2014 Immigration Report." 7 January 2015. http://www.ncsl.org/research/immigration/2014-immigration-report.aspx

14. National Conference of State Legislatures (NCSL). "2015 Immigration Report." 3 August 2015. http://www.ncsl.org/research/immigration/2015-immigration-report.aspx

15. California Legislative Information. Senate Bill No. 54. Chapter 495. https://leginfo.legislature.ca.gov/faces/billNavClient.xhtml?bill_id=201720180SB54

16. Ulloa, Jazmine Ulloa. "Nearly $50 million in the California state budget will go to expanded legal services for immigrants." *Los Angeles Times.* 15 June 2017. http://www.latimes.com/politics/essential/la-pol-ca-essential-politics-updates-nearly-50-million-in-the-california-1497576640-htmlstory.html

17. Silicon Valley Indicators. "Net Migration Flows: Foreign and Domestic Migration Santa Clara and San Mateo Counties."

http://siliconvalleyindicators.org/data/people/talent-flows-diversity/net-migration-flows/http://siliconvalleyindicators.org/data/people/talent-flows-diversity/net-migration-flows/

18. Public Policy Institute of California. "Undocumented Immigrants in California." March 2017. http://www.ppic.org/publication/undocumented-immigrants-in-california/

19. Massaro, Rachel and Jennings, Jill Minnick. "2017 Silicon Valley Index." op.cit.

20. Ibid.

21. Ibid.

22. Simmonds, Charlotte. "The Silicon Valley paradox: one in four people are at risk of hunger," *The Guardian*, 12 Dec. 12 2017. www.theguardian.com/us-news/2017/dec/12/the-silicon-valley-paradox-one-in-four-people-are-at-risk-of-hunger?CMP=share_btn_tw

23. Weller, Chris. "Silicon Valley's 'prosperity paradox' explains how 76,000 millionaires and billionaires fail to fix local problems." *Business Insider.* 22 Dec. 2016. www.businessinsider.com/silicon-valleys-prosperity-paradox-explained-2016-12

24. Solnit, Rebecca. "Diary." from the London Review of Books, Vol. 35. No. 3, 7 February 2013. Pp. 34-35. https://www.lrb.co.uk/v35/n03/rebecca-solnit/diary

25. Massaro. Op cit.

26. Not an exclusive problem of Silicon Valley. In fact, across the country, women's labor participation has plateaued in recent years. Fry, Richard and Stepler, Renee. "Women may never make up half of the U.S. workforce." Pew Research Center—Facttank, 31 January 2017. www.pewresearch.org/fact-tank/2017/01/31/women-may-never-make-up-half-of-the-u-s-workforce/.

27. The term, disruptive innovation, was introduced by Harvard Professor Clayton Christesen in the 1997 book *The Innovator's Dilemma* to explain how cheaper, simpler or unexpected products can compete and bring down big companies.

28. McShane, Sveta and Dorrier, Jason. "Ray Kurzweil Predicts Three Technologies Will Define Our Future," Singularity

Hub, 19 April 2016. https://singularityhub.com/2016/04/19/ray-kurzweil-predicts-three-technologies-will-define-our-future/.

29. "Why it Pays to Invest in Gender Diversity." Morgan Stanley. 11 May 2016. www.morganstanley.com/ideas/gender-diversity-investment-framework.

30. Hunt, Vivian., Layton, Dennis and Price, Sara. "Why Diversity Matters." McKinsey & Company. January 2015. www.mckinsey.com/business-functions/organization/our-insights/why-diversity-matters.

31. Lee, Linda-Eling et al. "Women on Boards: Global Trends in Gender Diversity on Corporate Boards." MSCI. November 2015. www.msci.com/documents/10199/04b6f646-d638-4878-9c61-4eb91748a82b

32. Ibid.

33. Noland, Marcus., Moran, Tyler and Kotschwar, Barbara. "Is Gender Diversity Profitable? Evidence from a Global Survey." Working Paper Series, 16-3. February 2016. https://piie.com/publications/wp/wp16-3.pdf

34. "Women in the Economy II: How Implementing a Women's Economic Empowerment Agenda Can Shape the Global Economy." Citi GPS Perspectives and Solutions. November 2017. https://ir.citi.com/rxehymXStWqV7Y6S58ExJLPdJPjqZicwdoxqT%2Fc0qDsBMFxbL%2FzcJiG%2FgKE%2BRxwHcad8oQrgD1w%3D

35. "The Illusion of Asian Success: Scant Progress for Minorities in Cracking the Glass Ceiling from 2007-2015." Ascend Foundation. 2015. http://c.ymcdn.com/sites/www.ascendleadership.org/resource/resmgr/research/TheIllusionofAsianSuccess.pdf

36. DuMonthier, Asha., Childers, Chandra and Milli, Jessica. "The Status of Black Women in the United States." Institute for Women's Policy Research, 2017. https://www.domesticworkers.org/sites/default/files/SOBW_report2017_compressed.pdf

37. Massaro. op.cit.

38. "Why Diversity Matters." Op.cit.

39.   See, Frey, William H. "Diversity defines the millennial generation." Brookings, 28 June 2016. https://www.brookings.edu/blog/the-avenue/2016/06/28/diversity-defines-the-millennial-generation/ Retrieved

40.   Health, United States, 2016. Available at: https://www.cdc.gov/nchs/data/hus/hus16.pdf

41.   Ibid.

42.   Cohn, D'Vera and Caumont, Andrea. "10 Demographic trends that are shaping the U.S. and the world." Pew Research Center. 31 March 2016. http://www.pewresearch.org/fact-tank/2016/03/31/10-demographic-trends-that-are-shaping-the-u-s-and-the-world/

43.   This quote was attributed to Sundar Pichai in "Silicon Valley, a Male Bastion?" by Vidula Chopra Rastogi. *Little India*, 17 November 2017. https://littleindia.com/silicon-valley-male-bastion/

44.   "Accelerating Acceptance 2017: A Harris Poll survey of American's acceptance of LGBTQ people." GLAAD, 2017. http://www.glaad.org/files/aa/2017_GLAAD_Accelerating_Acceptance.pdf

45.   Herbenick, Debby and Baldwin, Aleta. "What Each of Facebook's 51 New Gender Options Means." *The Daily Beast*. 15 February 2014. https://www.thedailybeast.com/what-each-of-facebooks-51-new-gender-options-means

46.   Clarke-Billings, Lucy. "What do Tinder's 37 New Gender Identity Options Mean?" *Newsweek*. 18 November 2016. http://www.newsweek.com/what-do-tinders-37-new-gender-identity-options-mean-522679 See also, Tinder #AllTypesAllSwipes official blog post, "Introducing More Genders on Tinder", 15 November 2016. http://blog.gotinder.com/genders/

47.   James, S. E., Herman, J. L., Rankin, S., Keisling, M., Mottet, L., & Anafi, M. "The Report of the 2015 U.S. Transgender Survey." National Center for Transgender Equality. Washington D.C., 2016. https://transequality.org/sites/default/files/docs/usts/USTS-Full-Report-Dec17.pdf

48.   Buck, Sebastian. "As Millennials Demand More Meaning, Older Brands Are Not Aging Well." *FastCompany*, 5 October 2017. www.fastcompany.com/40477211/as-millennials-demand-more-meaning-older-brands-are-not-aging-well

49.   Schnzenbach, Diane W., Nunn, Ryan., Bauer, Lauren and Breitwieser, Audrey. "The Closing of the Jobs Gap: A decade of recession and recovery."The Hamilton Project. Brookings. 4 August 2017.   https://www.brookings.edu/research/the-closing-of-the-jobs-gap-a-decade-of-recession-and-recovery/

50.   Adichi, Chimamanda Ngozi. "The danger of a single story." TEDGlobal   2009.   https://www.ted.com/talks/chimamanda_adichie_the_danger_of_a_single_story

A Network of Faults: How Education is Keeping Women Out of Tech

1.   Cimpian, Sarah J.R., Timmer,   Jennifeer D., Makowski, Martha B. and Miller, Emily K. "Have Gender Gaps in Math Closed? Achievement, Teacher Perceptions, and Learning Behaviors Across Two ECLS-K Cohorts." *American Educational Research Association* (AERA), 26 October 2016. http://journals.sagepub.com/doi/abs/10.1177/2332858416673617

2.   Lang Chen et al. "Positive Attitude Toward Math Supports Early Academic Success: Behavioral Evidence and Neurocognitive Mechanisms." *Psychological Science*. 24 January 2018. http://journals.sagepub.com/doi/full/10.1177/0956797617735528

3.   Hyde, Janet S., Lindberg, Sara M., Linn, Marcia C., Ellis, Amy B. and Williams, Caroline C. "Gender Similarities Characterize Math Performance." *Science*, Vol 321 (5888), 25 July 2008. http://science.sciencemag.org/content/321/5888/494

4.   "State of Girls and Women in STEM." National Girls Collaborative Project. 2017 https://negcproject.org/statistics.

5.   "Some well-meaning statements can spread stereotypes, new Stanford study says", *Stanford News*, 10 July 2018. https://

news.stanford.edu/2018/07/10/well-meaning-statements-can-spread-stereotypes-unintentionally/

6.   Sarah T. Lubienski, Joseph P. Robinson, Corinna C. Crane and Colleen M. Ganley. "Girls' and Boys' Mathematics Achievement, Affect, and Experiences: Findings from ECLS-K." *Journal for Research in Mathematics Education*, Vol 44 (4), July 2013, pp. 634-645. https://pdfs.semanticscholar.org/ce06/5a42930fc3d7d533b3 50877ebc19ce79e9e9.pdf

7. Margolis, Jane and Fisher, Allan. "Geek mythology and attracting undergraduate women to computer science. Impacting Change through Collaboration." Carnegie Mellon University, School of Computer Science. Joint National Conference of the Women in Engineering Program Advocates Network and the National Association of Minority Engineering Program Administrators, 1997. https://www.cs.cmu.edu/afs/cs/project/ gendergap/www/papers/wepan97.html

8.   See the OpEd Project at https://www.theopedproject.org/

9.   Guynn, Jessica. "CES fail: No women keynote addresses triggers backlash." *USA Today*. 5 January 2018. https://www.usatoday.com/ story/tech/2018/01/05/ces-women-diversity-keynote-speakers/1005021001/

10. Macharia, Sarah. "Who Makes the News?" Global Media Monitoring Project. 2015. http://cdn.agilitycms.com/ who-makes-the-news/Imported/reports_2015/global/gmmp_ global_report_en.pdf

11.   See, Women in Hollywood site available at: https://www. womenandhollywood.com/

12.   See, for example, Boys and Girls Clubs of America and Girls Who Code initiatives to reach students through Microsoft YouthSpark program.

13. "Girls Teaching Girls to Code." Stanford Office of Science Outreach. https://oso.stanford.edu/programs/209-girls-teaching-girls-to-code

14.   "State of Girls and Women in STEM." Op.cit.

15. Ibid.

16. Cavallaro, Mara. "Strength in Diversity: Where M-A Falls Short." *M-A Chronicle*. 7 September 2017. www.machronicle.com/strengthening-diversity-where-m-a-falls-short/

17. "The Majority Report." The Education Trust-West. 2017. https://29v0kg31gs803wndhe1sj1hd-wpengine.netdna-ssl.com/wp-content/uploads/sites/3/2015/11/ETW_MajorityReport.FINAL-11.3.17.pdf

18. Bell, Alex., Chetty, Raj., Jaravel, Xavier., Petkova, Neviana and Van Reenen, John. "Who Becomes an Inventor in America? The Importance of Exposure to Innovation." December 2017. www.equality-of-opportunity.org/assets/documents/inventors_paper.pdf

19. "The Majority Report." Op.cit.

20. Melissa Korn, "How Much Does Being a Legacy Help Your College Admissions Odds?" *The Wall Street Journal*, July 9, 2014. www.wsj.com/articles/legacy-preferences-complicate-colleges-diversity-push-1531128601

21. Ashkenas, Jeremy., Park, Haeyoun and Pearce, Adam. "Even with Affirmative Action, Blacks and Hispanics Are More Underrepresented at Top Colleges Than 35 Years Ago." *The New York Times*. 24 August 2017. https://www.nytimes.com/interactive/2017/08/24/us/affirmative-action.html

22. Ashkenas, Jeremy et al. Op.cit.

23. "Bachelor's degrees awarded, by race or ethnicity, citizenship, sex, and field: 2012." Table 5-7. National Science Foundation Data. www.nsf.gov/statistics/2017/nsf17310/data.cfm

24. OCDE. "2015 Science, Technology and Industry Scoreboard Report: Innovation for Growth and Society." OECD Publishing. http://dx.doi.org/10.1787/sti_scoreboard-2015-en and "National Science Board, Science and Engineering Indicators 2016." https://nsf.gov/statistics/2016/nsb20161/#/

25. Margolis, Jane and Fisher, Allan. Op.cit.

26. STEMINIST.com

27.   Wynn, Alison T. and Correll, Shelley J. "Gendered Perceptions of Cultural and Skill Alignment in Technology Companies," *Soc. Sci.* MDPI, 2017. file:///C:/Users/nade_marques/Downloads/socsci-06-00045.pdf

28.   Staley, Oliver. "Harvey Mudd College took on gender bias and now more than half its computer science majors are women." *Quartz.* 22 August 2016. https://qz.com/730290/harvey-mudd-college-took-on-gender-bias-and-now-more-than-half-its-computer-science-majors-are-women/

29.   Staley, Oliver. Op.cit.

30.   Pedersen, Kristine. "The Clayman Institute Takes Aim at the STEM Pipeline with Its New "Seeds of Change" Program." *Gender News.* The Clayman Institute. 30 November 2017. http://gender.stanford.edu/news/2017/clayman-institute-takes-aim-stem-pipeline-its-new-%E2%80%9Cseeds-change%E2%80%9D-program

31.   McBride, Sarah. "Computer science now top major for women at Stanford University." *Reuters.* 9 October 2015. www.reuters.com/article/us-women-technology-stanford/computer-science-now-top-major-for-women-at-stanford-university-idUSKCN0S32F020151009

32.   St. Fleur, Nicholas. "Many Women Leave Engineering, Blame the Work Culture." *NPR.* All tech considered. 12 August 2014. https://www.npr.org/sections/alltechconsidered/2014/08/12/339638726/many-women-leave-engineering-blame-the-work-culture

33.   Kugler, Adriana D., Tinsley, Catherine H., Ukhaneva, Olga. "Choice of Majors: Are Women Really Different from Men?" NBER Working Paper No. 23735. The National Bureau of Economic Research. August 2017. http://www.nber.org/papers/w23735

34.   Reskin, Barbara. "What's the difference?" in "The Difference 'difference' makes: women and leadership." Edited by Deborah L. Rhode. Stanford University Press. 2003.

35.   Reskin, Barbara. Op.cit.

36. Ballen, Cissy J., Salehi, Shima and Cotner, Sehoya. "Exams disadvantage women in introductory biology." *PLOS*. 19 October 2017. http://journals.plos.org/plosone/article?id=10.1371/journal.pone.0186419

37. Sloan, Elizabeth. "Conference celebrates, illuminates women leading the way in science." SCOPE. Stanford Medicine. 31 October 2017. http://scopeblog.stanford.edu/2017/10/31/conference-celebrates-illuminates-women-leading-the-way-in-science/

38. Craig, A. "Peer mentoring female computing students: Does it make a difference?" In Proceedings of the 3rd Austrailasian Conference on Computer Science Education (ACSE '98). ACM, 1998, New York, pp. 41-47. https://dl.acm.org/citation.cfm?id=289401

39. Dennehy, Tara C. and Dasgupta, Nilanjana. "Female peer mentors early in college increase women's positive academic experiences and retention in engineering." *PNAS*, 6 June 2017. Vol. 114 (23). www.pnas.org/content/114/23/5964.long

40. Byrne, Kelly Z. "The Roles of Campus-Based Women's Centers." *Feminist Teacher*. Vo.13, no. 1, 2000, pp. 48-60.

41. Bryant, Alyssa N. "Changes in Attitudes Toward Women's Roles: Predicting Gender-Role Traditionalism Among College Students." *Sex Roles*. February 2003, Vol. 48 (3-4), pp. 131-142. https://link.springer.com/article/10.1023/A%3A1022451205292

42. Lovejoy. Meg, "'You can't go home again:' The Impact of Women's Studies on Intellectual and Personal Development." *NWSA Journal*, 1998, pp. 119-38.

43. See, Butler, D. M., and Christensen, R. "Mixing and matching: The effect on student performance of teaching assistants of the same gender." *Political Science and Politics*, 2003, 36(4), 781-786. And Robst, J., Keil, J., and Russo, D. "The effect of gender composition of faculty on student retention." *Economics of Education Review*, 1998, 29(4), 429-439.

44. Silbey, Susan S. "Why Do So Many Women Who Study Engineering Leave the Field?" *Harvard Business Review*. 23 August 2016. https://hbr.org/2016/08/why-do-so-many-women-who-study-engineering-leave-the-field

45. "Stanford Facts 2017: A look at Stanford University Today." Stanford University. 2017. http://facts.stanford.edu/pdf/StanfordFacts_2017.pdf

46. "Taskforce Women in Leadership: Findings and Recommendations." Stanford University. September 2016. https://provost.stanford.edu/wp-content/uploads/sites/4/2016/12/Taskforce_WomeninLeadership-2.pdf

47. "Digest of Education Statistics: 2015 Tables and Figures." National Center for Educational Statistics. https://nces.ed.gov/programs/digest/d15/tables/dt15_325.45.asp

48. Weisshaar, Katherine. "Publish and Perish? An Assessment of Gender Gap in Promotion to Tenure in Academia." *Social Forces*, Volume 96 (2), December 2017. PP 529-560. https://academic.oup.com/sf/article-abstract/96/2/529/3897008?redirectedFrom=fulltext

49. Ibid.

50. Milkman, Katherine L., Akinola, Modupe and Chugh, Dolly. "What happens before?" *Journal of Applied Psychology*, Vol 100 (6), 2015.

51. Ibid.

52. Boring, Anne., Ottoboni, Kellie and Stark, Philip. "Student Evaluations of Teaching (Mostly) Do Not Measure Teaching Effectiveness." *ScienceOpen Research*. 1 July 2016. https://www.scienceopen.com/document?id=0bc459de-6f8f-487f-b925-863834a74048

53. Milkman, Katherine L. et. al. Op. cit.

54. "UIS Fact Sheet: Women in Science." UNESCO Institute of Statistics, 2017. http://uis.unesco.org/en/topic/women-science

55. Williams, Nancy. "Estelle Freedman win long battle for tenure", *The Stanford Daily*, 26 September 1986. https://stanforddailyarchive.com/cgi-bin/stanford?a=d&d=stanford19830926-01.2.3

56. "4.8 Million College Students are Raising Children." Institute for Women's Policy Research. Fact Sheet. November

2014. https://iwpr.org/wp-content/uploads/wpallimport/files/iwpr-export/publications/C424_Student%20Parents_final.pdf

57. Ibid.

58. "Supporting women's success in academic research careers." *News*. Harvard School of Public Health (HSPH). 21 Sept. 2017.

59. Cantalupo, Nancy Chi and Kidder, William C. "A Systematic Look at a Serial Problem: Sexual Harassment of Students by University Faculty." *Utah Law Review*, Forthcoming, May 2017.

60. Druy, Emily. "Stanford: Sexual misconduct revelation exposes storied professor's secret." *The Mercury News*. 30 November 2017. www.mercurynews.com/2017/11/30/stanford-sexual-misconduct-revelation-exposes-storied-professors-secret/ See also, "Two women accuse former Stanford professors of sexual assault." *The Stanford Daily*. 9 November 2017. www.stanforddaily.com/2017/11/09/two-women-accuse-former-stanford-professors-of-sexual-assault/

61. Ibid.

62. Flaherty, Colleen. "Putting Harassers on Notice." *Inside Higher Ed*. 15 October 2015. https://www.insidehighered.com/news/2015/10/15/berkeley-astronomer-resigns-over-sexual-harassment-investigation See also, Kimberly Latta accusations against History and English Professor Franco Moretti in "Retired English professor accused of sexual assault by former graduate student." *The Stanford Daily*. 9 November 2017. www.stanforddaily.com/2017/11/09/english-professor-accused-of-sexual-assault-by-former-graduate-student/

63. Silbey, Susan S. "Why Do So Many Women Who Study Engineering Leave the Field?" *Harvard Business Review*. 23 August 2016. https://hbr.org/2016/08/why-do-so-many-women-who-study-engineering-leave-the-field

64. RAINN. "Campus Sexual Violence: Statistics." 2016. http://time.com/5047213/brock-turner-rape-trial-appeal-conviction/

65. "33 reports of rape on Stanford campus in 2016, sexual assault on the rise." *KTVU*, Palo Alto, 29 September, 2017. http://www.ktvu.com/news/33-reports-of-rape-on-stanford-campus-in-2016-sexual-assault-on-the-rise

66. "What is Uniform Crime Reporting." City of Palo Alto Crime Statistics. www.cityofpaloalto.org/gov/depts/pol/info/stats.asp

67. "Progress report from Provost Persis Drell to the campus community on Student Title IX Process." *Stanford Report*. 31 May 2017. https://news.stanford.edu/2017/05/31/progress-report-student-title-ix-process/

68. Letter by Provost Persis Drell, "Stanford's Resolution Agreement with OCR.", Notes from the Quad. Stanford University, 10 April 2018. https://quadblog.stanford.edu/2018/04/10/stanfords-resolution-agreement-with-ocr/

69. Meixler, Eli. "Brock Turner Is Trying to Get His Sexual Assault Convictions Overturned." *TIME*, 4 December 2017. http://time.com/5047213/brock-turner-rape-trial-appeal-conviction/

70. California Penal Code—PEN 261. http://codes.findlaw.com/ca/penal-code/pen-sect-261.html

71. Hayward, Brad. "Sexual violence prevention programs continue evolving, expanding." *Stanford Report*. 3 November 2017. https://news.stanford.edu/2017/11/03/sexual-violence-prevention-programs/

Stanford: The Unicorn in the Room

1. "The Life and Times of a Victorian Lady: Jane Lathrop Stanford." *Sandstone & Tile*. Stanford Historical Society. Volume 21, No. 3. Summer 1997. https://sites.stanford.edu/Founders/sites/default/files/ST21no3.pdf

2. Sullivan, Kathleen J. "'Let us be fearless.' Stanford President Marc Tessier-Lavigne tells university." *Stanford News*. 21 October 2016. https://news.stanford.edu/2016/10/21/let-us-fearless-president-marc-tessier-lavigne-tells-university/

3. "Stanford Facts 2017." Administration and Finances. http://facts.stanford.edu/administration/finances

4. Unicorn is a startup company valued at more than a billion dollars, typically in the tech industry.

5. "A History of Stanford." Stanford University. https://www.stanford.edu/about/history/

6. Federal Telegraph was originally called Poulson Wireless Telephone and Telegraph Company. See, Eesley, Charles E. and Miller, William F. "Impact: Stanford University's Economic Impact via Innovation and Entrepreneurship." 16 October 2017. https://papers.ssrn.com/sol3/papers.cfm?abstract_id=2227460

7. Eesley, Charles E. and Miller, William F. Op.cit.

8. Sun Microsystems' name is an acronym for Stanford University Network, the campus' computer system in 1982. Paypal cofounder, Peter Thiel graduated from Stanford Law School in 1992.

9. Eesley, Charles E. and Miller, William F. Op.cit.

10. Ibid.

11. Hobbs, Allyson and Satia, Priya. "An Academic Conference Featured 30 White Men and One White Woman. How Should the University Respond?" *The Washington Post*, 26 March2018. www.washingtonpost.com/news/made-by-history/wp/2018/03/26/an-academic-conference-featured-only-white-men-how-should-the-university-respond/?utm_term=.150e4d1d01e5

12. Contreras, Brian. "Leaked emails show Hoover academic conspiring with College Republicans to conduct 'opposition research' on student." *The Stanford Daily*, 1 June2018. www.stanforddaily.com/2018/05/31/emails-between-ferguson-scr-reveal-opposition-research-against-ocon-prompt-fergusons-resignation-from-cardinal-conversations-leadership-role/

13. 2001—Carly Fiorina, former CEO for Hewlett-Packard; 2002 Condoleezza Rice; 2004 Sandra Day O'Connor; 2008 Oprah Winfrey; 2010 Susan Rice; 2014 Melinda Gates shared the stage and address with Bill Gates.

14. "Taskforce Women in Leadership: Findings and Recommendations." Stanford University. September 2016. https://provost.stanford.edu/wp-content/uploads/sites/4/2016/12/Taskforce_WomeninLeadership-2.pdf

15. California is one of the states with the highest participation of women in Fortune 1000 companies (20.8%) and in 2017, women constituted 18.8% of Fortune 1000 technology companies' boards. See, 2017 Gender Diversity Index Key Findings 20% by 2020 Women on Boards. www.2020wob.com/companies/2020-gender-diversity-index

16. "Women CEOs of the S&P 500." Catalyst. Knowledge Center. www.catalyst.org/knowledge/women-ceos-sp-500

17. "2017 Gender Diversity Index Key Findings. 20% by 2020 Women on Boards." https://www.2020wob.com/companies/2020-gender-diversity-index

18. Apple's Inclusion and Diversity Report is available at: https://www.apple.com/diversity/

19. Cao, Sissi. "A Data-Backed Look Into Silicon Valley's Gender Equity Problem," *Observer.* 16 Nov 2017. http://observer.com/2017/11/a-data-backed-look-into-silicon-valleys-gender-equality-problem/

20. Some of the notorious examples of negative leadership are William Shafter, inventor of the silicon transistor, in 1956, who was a proponent of eugenics and a racist submitting his employees to lie detectors among other bizarre and unacceptable behavior. See, Berlin, Leslie. "Troublemakers: Silicon Valley Coming of Age." Simon & Schuster. 2017.

21. Research has shown that women apologize more frequently because men have a higher threshold for what constitutes offensive behavior. In other words, men rate their offenses as less severe than women. See, Schumann, Karina and Ross, Michael. "Why Women Apologize More Thank Men: Gender Differences in Thresholds for Perceiving Offensive Behavior." *Psychological Science.* April 2010.

22. Jong, Anneke. "Why We Need to Rethink Women in Tech," *The Muse, Tools and Skills.* No Date. www.themuse.com/advice/why-we-need-to-rethink-women-in-tech

23. Fairchild, Caroline "Investors and startup founders think tech's diversity problem will solve itself," featured in Editor's Picks, *Entrepreneurship, VC & Private Equity.*

Linkedln. 3 Nov. 2016. www.linkedin.com/pulse/startup-founders-investors-think-techs-diversity-solve-fairchild/

24. Johnson, Stefanie K. J. and Hekman, David R. "Women and Minorities are Penalized for Promoting Diversity," *Harvard Business Review*. 23 March 2016.

25. Rickman, Pamela. "Stiletto Network: Inside the Women's Power Circles That Are Changing the Face of Business." AMACOM. 2013.

26. Paquette, Danielle. "In a first, only women will lead Davos—an elite meeting of mostly men." *The Washington Post* and *SFGate*. 22 January 2018. http://www.sfgate.com/news/article/In-a-first-only-women-will-lead-Davos-an-elite-12514458.php

27. Ballakrishen, Swethaa. Fielding-Singh, Priya and Magliozzi, Devon. "Intentional Invisibility: Professional Women and the Navigation of Workplace Constraints", *Sociological Perspectives*. 25 June2018. http://journals.sagepub.com/doi/pdf/10.1177/0731121418782185

28. "2017 Edelman Trust Barometer Reveals Global Implosion of Trust." Eldman Trust. 15 January 2017. https://www.edelman.com/news/2017-edelman-trust-barometer-reveals-global-implosion/

29. Cross, Rob., Rebele, Reb and Grant, Adam. "Collaborative Overload." *Harvard Business Review*. January-February 2016 Issue. https://hbr.org/2016/01/collaborative-overload

30. Freeman, Jo. "The Tyranny of Structurelessness." *Berkeley Journal of Sociology*. Vol. 17, 1972-73, pp. 151-164. https://www.jstor.org/stable/41035187

Women's Tech Dilemma

1. Hewlett, Syvia A., Luce, Carolyn B., Servon, Lisa J. and Sherbin, Laura. "The Athena Factor: Reversing the Brain Drain in Science, Engineering and Technology." *Harvard Business Review*. Research Report. 22 May 2008. https://hbr.org/product/the-athena-factor-reversing-the-brain-drain-in-science-engineering-and-technology/10094-PDF-ENG

2.   Wynn, Alison T. and Correll, Shelley J. "Gendered Perceptions of Cultural and Skill Alignment in Technology Companies," *Soc. Sci.* MDPI, 2017. file:///C:/Users/nade_marques/Downloads/socsci-06-00045.pdf

3.   Scott, Allison., Klein, Freada K. and Onovakpuri, Uriridiakoghene. "The Leavers Study: A first-of-its-kind analysis of why people voluntarily left jobs in tech." Kapur Center for Social Impact. 27 April 2017. www.kaporcenter.org/wp-content/uploads/2017/04/KAPOR_Tech-Leavers-17-0427.pdf

4.   See, for example, Megan Molteni and Adam Rogers rebuttal of James Damore Google Memo in "The Actual Science of James Damore Google Memo," *Wired*, 15 August 2017. www.wired.com/story/the-pernicious-science-of-james-damores-google-memo/ Also in https://gizmodo.com/exclusive-heres-the-full-10-page-anti-diversity-screed-1797564320

5.   Parker, Kim and Funk, Cary. "Gender Discrimination comes in many forms for today's working women." Pew Research Center. 14 Dec. 2017. www.pewresearch.org/fact-tank/2017/12/14/gender-discrimination-comes-in-many-forms-for-todays-working-women/

6.   Funk, Cary and Parker, Kim. "Women and Men in STEM Often at Odds Over Workplace Equity." Pew Research Center. 9 January 2018. www.pewsocialtrends.org/2018/01/09/women-and-men-in-stem-often-at-odds-over-workplace-equity/

7.   "Women Who Code." Tech and Startup Survey. August 2017. www.womenwhotech.com/resources/tech-and-startup-culture-survey.

8.   See, Susan Fowler blog post alleging that Uber's human-resources systematically ignored her reports of sexism and sexual harassment. Available at: https://www.susanjfowler.com/blog/2017/2/19/reflecting-on-one-very-strange-year-at-uber.

9.   Kosoff, Maya. "Mass Firing at Uber as Sexual Scandal Grows." *Vanity Fair.* 6 June 2017. www.vanityfair.com/news/2017/06/uber-fires-20-employees-harassment-investigation. After the sexual scandals, David Bonderman, Uber board member, resigned after sexist remarks at the company's meeting. Isaac, Mike and

Chira, Susan. "David Bonderman Resigns From Uber Board After Sexist Remark." *The New York Times*, 13 June 2017. www. nytimes.com/2017/06/13/technology/uber-sexual-harassment-huffington-bonderman.html.

10. "The Tech Industry Gender Discrimination Problem." *The New Yorker*. 20 Nov. 2017. www.newyorker.com/magazine/2017/11/20/the-tech-industrys-gender-discrimination-problem

11. Kay, Katty and Shipman, Claire. "The Confidence Code: The Science and Art of Self-Assurance—What Women Should Know." HarperCollins Publishers. April 2015.

12. See, Textio.com

13. Koh, Yoree. "How Language in Job Listings Could Widen Silicon Valley's Gender Divide." *The Wall Street Journal*. 13 Dec. 2017. www.wsj.com/articles/how-language-in-job-listings-could-widen-silicon-valleys-gender-divide-1513189821

14. Andrews, TL. "Just a few words can increase female and minority job applicants by more than 20%." *Quartz*. 11 July 2017. https://qz.com/1023518/just-a-few-words-can-increase-female-and-minority-job-applicants-by-over-20/

15. Wong, Julia C. "Women considered better coders—but only if they hide their gender." *The Guardian*. 12 February 2016. www.theguardian.com/technology/2016/feb/12/women-considered-better-coders-hide-gender-github

16. Weingarten, Elizabeth. "Why Pretending You Don't See Race or Gender Is an Obstacle to Equality." Better Life Lab. 23 May 2017. www.slate.com/blogs/better_life_lab/2017/05/23/you_re_not_blind_to_race_and_gender_but_your_hiring_process_can_be.html

17. "Most frequent biases in business" *McKinsey Quarterly*, from Finkelstein, Sydney., Whitehead, Jo and Campbell, Andrew. "Think Again: Why Good Leaders Make Bad Decisions and How to Keep It from Happening to You." Harvard Business Press. Boston. 2008.

18. "Ten stats that prove Silicon Valley hasn't fixed its diversity problem." TechCo, 25 June 2018. https://tech.co/stats-silicon-valley-fixed-diversity-problem-2018-06

19. "Ten stats that prove Silicon Valley hasn't fixed its diversity problem." Op. cit.

20. Dizard, John. "Some gender imbalances are in the genes." *Financial Times.* 14 December 2017. www.ft.com/content/e2dd5536-e0b2-11e7-8f9f-de1c2175f5ce

21. "Google finally discloses its diversity record, and it's not good." *PBS News Hour.* Nation. 28 May 2014. www.pbs.org/newshour/nation/google-discloses-workforce-diversity-data-good

22. Beer, Michael., Finnstrom, Magnus and Schrader, Derek. "The Great Training Robbery." Harvard Business School Working Paper 16-121. 21 April 2016. www.hbs.edu/faculty/Publication%20Files/16-121_bc0f03ce-27de-4479-a90e-9d78b8da7b67.pdf

23. Correll, Shelley. "SWS 2016 Feminist Lecture: Reducing Gender Biases in Modern Workplaces: A small wins approach to organizational change." *Sage Journals.* Vol. 31(6), 2017.

24. DuMonthier, Asha., Childers, Chandra and Milli, Jessica. "The Status of Black Women in the United States." Institute for Women's Policy Research. 2017. www.domesticworkers.org/sites/default/files/SOBW_report2017_compressed.pdf

25. "3 in 5 Employees Did Not Negotiate Salary." *Glassdoor Updates.* 2 May 2016. www.glassdoor.com/blog/3-5-u-s-employees-negotiate-salary/

26. Ibid.

27. Tiku, Nitasha. "Google Deliberately Confuses Its Employees, FED Says." *Wired.* 25 July 2017. www.wired.com/story/google-department-of-labor-gender-pay-lawsuit/

28. Kolhatkar, Sheelah. "The Tech Industry Gender Discrimination Problem." *The New Yorker.* 20 Nov. 2017. www.newyorker.com/magazine/2017/11/20/the-tech-industrys-gender-discrimination-problem

29. Ibid.

30. Naughton, Eileen. "Our focus on pay equity." Google Blog Post. 11 April 2017. www.blog.google/topics/diversity/our-focus-pay-equity/

31. Kolhatkar, Sheelah. Op. cit.

32. Morris, David Z. "Tech's Gender Pay Gap Hits Younger Women Hardest", *Fortune.* 27 January 2017. http://fortune.com/2017/01/22/techs-gender-pay-gap-young-women/

33. Mulvaney, Erin. "EEOC Fights Ninth Circuit Ruling That 'Institutionalizes' Gender Pay Gap." *The National Law Journal.* 23 May 2017.

34. Ibid.

35. Assembly Bill No. 168. Chapter 688. Approved by Governor Jerry Brown. 22 October 2017. https://leginfo.legislature.ca.gov/faces/billTextClient.xhtml?bill_id=201720180AB168

36. Garcia-Alonso, Jennifer., Krentz, Matt., Taplett, Frances B., Tracey, Claire and Tsusaka, Mikki. "Getting the Most from Your Diversity Dollars." BCG. 21 June 2017. www.bcg.com/publications/2017/people-organization-behavior-culture-getting-the-most-from-diversity-dollars.aspx

37. Budig, Michelle J. "The Fatherhood Bonus and The Motherhood Penalty: Parenthood and the Gender Gap in Pay." *Third Way.* 2 September 2014. http://www.thirdway.org/report/the-fatherhood-bonus-and-the-motherhood-penalty-parenthood-and-the-gender-gap-in-pay

38. "Gwilliam, Ivary, Chiosso, Cavalli & Brewer release the following: Prenatal genetic testing company accused of gender and pregnancy discrimination." *Cision PR Newswire*, 12 July 2018. www.prnewswire.com/news-releases/gwilliam-ivary-chiosso-cavalli—brewer-release-the-following-prenatal-genetic-testing-company-accused-of-gender-and-pregnancy-discrimination-300679897.html

39. Katz, Lawrence F. and Krueger, Alan B. "The Rise and Nature of Alternative Work Arrangements in the United States, 1995-2015." Princeton University and NBER. 29 March 2016. https://krueger.princeton.edu/sites/default/files/akrueger/files/katz_krueger_cws_-_march_29_20165.pdf

40. Schnzenbach, Diane W., Nunn, Ryan., Bauer, Lauren and Breitwieser, Audrey. "The Closing of the Jobs Gap: A decade of recession and recovery." The Hamilton Project.

Brookings. 4 August 2017. www.brookings.edu/research/the-closing-of-the-jobs-gap-a-decade-of-recession-and-recovery/

41. "Even side hustles pay men more than women including driving for uber", *Market Watch*. 26 June 2018. www.marketwatch.com/story/even-side-hustles-pay-men-more-than-womenincluding-driving-for-uber-2018-06-25.

42. Black, Sandra E., Schanzenbach, Diane W. and Breitwieser, Audrey. "The Recent Decline in Women's Labor Force Participation." In Schanzenbach, Diane W. and Nunn, Ryan. "The 51% Driving Growth through Women's Economic Participation." The Hamilton Project. Brookings. October 2017.

43. LaLumia, Sara. "Tax Policies to Encourage Women's Labor Force Participation." In Schanzenbach, Diane W. and Nunn, Ryan. Op. cit.

Let's Talk About Money: The VC and Startup Worlds

1. Lemke-Santangelo, Gretchen. "Abiding Courage: African American Migrant Women and the East Bay Community." University of North Carolina Press. 9 Nov. 2000.

2. MacLean, Eliza. "A Genealogy of Social Movements in the American West: The Spatial Occupation of the Military-Industrial Complex and its Effects on the Legacy of Activism." U.S. History Scene. http://ushistoryscene.com/article/westsocialmovements/

3. Lisa Berlin. Op.cit.

4. "Frequently Asked Questions." Small Business Administration. Advocacy: the voice of small business in government. https://www.sba.gov/sites/default/files/FAQ_Sept_2012.pdf

5. "Analysis of 2012 Survey of Business Owners Fact Sheet, Latina Women-Owned Businesses." National Women's Business Council. 2012. www.mbda.gov/sites/mbda.gov/files/migrated/files-attachments/Latina%20Women%20Entrepreneurs.pdf

6. Brown, Carolyn M. "Angels and Unicorns: Black Women-Owned Businesses Grow But Raise Very Little Seed Money." *Black Enterprise*. 29 February 2016. www.blackenterprise.com/

angels-and-unicorns-black-women-owned-businesses-grow-but-raise-very-little-seed-money/

7. "Analysis of 2012 Survey of Business Owners Fact Sheet, Latina Women-Owned Businesses." Op. cit.

8. For a list of largest women-owned businesses in Silicon Valley ranked by 2016 revenue see, Downey, Rosie. "Largest women-owned businesses in Silicon Valley." *Silicon Valley Business Journal.* 1 September 2017. www.stage4solutions.com/SVBJW.html

9. Shafrir, Doree. "Hundreds of People Told Us How Sexual Harassment In Tech Derailed Their Careers." *BuzzFeed News.* 7 December 2017. www.buzzfeed.com/doree/we-surveyed-hundreds-about-techs-harassment-problem?utm_term=.hcxyWB0Vnx#.imvD7xezgm

10. Teare, Gené., and Desmond, Ned. "The first comprehensive study on women in venture capital and their impact on female founders." TC Crunch Base Women in Venture Report. 19 April 2016. https://techcrunch.com/2016/04/19/the-first-comprehensive-study-on-women-in-venture-capital/

11. Zarya, Valentina. "Venture Capital's Funding Gender Gap Is Actually Getting Worse." *Fortune.* 13 March 2017. http://fortune.com/2017/03/13/female-founders-venture-capital/

12. Chang, Emily. "Oh My God, This is So F—Ed UP: Inside Silicon Valley's Secretive, Orgiastic Dark Side." *Vanityfair.* An adaptation of *Brotopia: Breaking Up the Boy's Club of Silicon Valley* in Vanity Fair. February 2018. https://www.vanityfair.com/news/2018/01/brotopia-silicon-valley-secretive-orgiastic-inner-sanctum

13. In California, employees have certain protections when working on a side project. One can use general knowledge, skills and experience gained through the course of ones employment as long as the invention is not substantially related to the employer's business or "anticipated research development." See, California Labor Code—LAB 96. http://codes.findlaw.com/ca/labor-code/lab-sect-96.html

14. See, Entis, Laura. "The Medical Research Gap That's Leaving Women's Health Startups Behind." *FastCompany.* 9 Nov.

2017. www.fastcompany.com/40490441/the-medical-research-gap-thats-leaving-womens-health-startups-behind

15. Malmstrom, Malin., Johansson, Jeaneth and Wincent, Joakim. "We recorded VCs conversations and analyzed how differently they talk about female entrepreneurs." *Harvard Business Review.* 17 May 2017. https://hbr.org/2017/05/we-recorded-vcs-conversations-and-analyzed-how-differently-they-talk-about-female-entrepreneurs.

16. Albergoti, Reed. "Investors Moving to Pull out of Binary." *The Information.* 26 Jun. 2017. www.theinformation.com/investors-moving-to-pull-out-of-binary.

17. Benner, Katie. "Women in Tech Speak Frankly on Culture of Harassment." *The New York Times.* 30 June 2017. www.nytimes.com/2017/06/30/technology/women-entrepreneurs-speak-out-sexual-harassment.html?_r=0

18. Dave McClure Blog post in Medium. "I'm a Creep. I'm Sorry." https://medium.com/@davemcclure/im-a-creep-i-m-sorry-d2c13e996ea0.

19. Kendall, Marisa. "New Bill would crack down on VC sexual harassment." *The Mercury News.* 17 August 2017. www.mercurynews.com/2017/08/17/exclusive-new-bill-would-explicitly-ban-vc-sexual-harassment/

20. Teare, Gené and Desmond, Ned. "The first comprehensive study on women in venture capital and their impact on female founders." TC Crunch Base Women in Venture Report. 19 April 2016. https://techcrunch.com/2016/04/19/the-first-comprehensive-study-on-women-in-venture-capital/

21. Cohen, Lisa E. and Broschak, Joseph B. "Whose Jobs Are These? The Impact of the Proportion of Female Managers on the Number of New Management Jobs Filled by Women versus Men." *Sage Journals*, Vol 58 (4), 2013. http://journals.sagepub.com/doi/abs/10.1177/0001839213504403

22. Kanze, Dana., Huang, Laura., Conley, Mark and Higgins, E. Tory. "Male and female entrepreneurs get asked different questions by VCs and it affects how much funding they get." *Harvard Business Review.* 27 June 2017. https://hbr.org/2017/06/

male-and-female-entrepreneurs-get-asked-different-questions-by-vcs-and-it-affects-how-much-funding-they-get

23. Sheryl Sandberg. Facebook Post from 3 Dec. 2017. www.facebook.com/sheryl/posts/10159569315265177

24. Siew, Walden. "Gender bias is a huge problem in workplace: Facebook Coo Sheryl Sandberg." 20 June 2018. www.employeebenefitadviser.com/news/facebook-sheryl-sandberg-says-gender-bias-is-a-huge-challenge?brief=00000152-146e-d1cc-a5fa-7cff8fee0000

25. Hoffman, Reid. "The Human Rights of Women Entrepreneurs." *LinkedIn*. 23 June 2017. www.linkedin.com/pulse/human-rights-women-entrepreneurs-reid-hoffman/

People Like Us: Can Solidarity and Giving Back Save Silicon Valley?

1. Brinklow, Adam. "Google expansion coming to Mountain View Headquarters." *Curbed*. 8 March 2017. https://sf.curbed.com/2017/3/8/14858200/google-headquarters-expansion-tech

2. Avalos, George. "How big can Google get? Its aggressive push for elbow room in the Bay Area." *The Mercury News*. 8 August 2017. www.mercurynews.com/2017/08/08/how-big-can-google-get-its-aggressive-push-for-elbow-room-in-the-bay-area/

3. Brinklow, Adam. "Apple campus to open in April." *Curbed*. 22 February 2017. https://sf.curbed.com/2017/2/22/14698816/apple-park-campus-opens

4. Krieger, Lisa M. "Stanford's expansion plans stir debate in congested Palo Alto." *The Mercury News*. 6 November 2017. www.mercurynews.com/2017/11/06/stanfords-expansion-plans-stir-debate-in-congested-palo-alto/

5. Har, Janie. "Silicon Valley's homeless: Everyday workers in shadow of tech affluence." *Associated Press and Mercury News*. 7 November 2017. www.mercurynews.com/2017/11/07/in-shadow-of-tech-boom-the-working-homeless-sleep-in-cars/

6. Solon, Olivia. "Ashamed to work in Silicon Valley: how techies became the new bankers." *The Guardian*. 8 November 2017. www.

theguardian.com/technology/2017/nov/08/ashamed-to-work-in-silicon-valley-how-techies-became-the-new-bankers

7. Auerhahn, Louise., Brownstein, Bob., Chavez, Cindy and Menon, Esha. "Life in the Valley Economy—Saving the Middle Class: Lessons from Silicon Valley—2012." Working Partnership USA. www.wpusa.org/Publication/LIVE2012-ExecSumm-web.pdf

8. "Poverty in the San Francisco Bay Area: Research Brief." Silicon Valley Institute for Regional Studies. March 2015. http://siliconvalleyindicators.org/pdf/poverty-brief-2015-03.pdf

9. Waters, Richard. "The great Silicon Valley land grab." *Financial Times*. 23 August 2017. www.ft.com/content/82bc282e-8790-11e7-bf50-e1c239b45787

10. "How many miles do Bay Area drivers travel in congestion?" Metropolitan Transportation Commission. Updated September 2017. http://www.vitalsigns.mtc.ca.gov/miles-traveled-congestion

11. "Living in Vehicles and Homeless Information. Study, Survey and Strategy." City of Mountain View. www.mountainview.gov/depts/comdev/preservation/living_in_vehicles_and_homeless_information.asp

12. Dettling, Lisa J. and Kearney, Melissa S. "House prices and birth rates: The impact of the real estate market on the decision to have a baby." *Journal of Public Economics*. Vol. 10, February 2014. pp. 82-100. www.sciencedirect.com/science/article/pii/S0047272713001904

13. Kater, Charlene K., Billhardt, Kris A., Warren, Joseph., Rollins, Chiquita and Glass, Nancy E. "Domestic violence, housing instability, and homelessness: A review of the policies and program practices for meeting the needs of survivors." *Aggression and Violent Behavior*. Vol. 15, 2010. pp. 430-439. http://b.3cdn.net/naeh/416990124d53c2f67d_72m6b5uib.pdf

14. "Domestic Violence and Housing: A Manual and Toolkit for California Advocates." The National Housing Law Project. 2009. www.nhlp.org/files/NHLP%20Domestic%20Violence%20&%20Housing%20Manual.pdf

15. "QuickFacts. East Palo Alto city." United States Census Bureau. www.census.gov/quickfacts/fact/table/eastpaloaltocitycalifornia,US/PST045217

16. "Bay Area Census." City of East Palo Alto. San Mateo County. www.bayareacensus.ca.gov/cities/EastPaloAlto.htm

17. Gee, Alastair. "More than one-third of schoolchildren are homeless in shadow of Silicon Valley." *The Guardian.* 28 December 2016. www.theguardian.com/society/2016/dec/28/silicon-valley-homeless-east-palo-alto-california-schools

18. Auerhahn, Louise., Brownstein, Bob., Chavez, Cindy and Menon, Esha. Op.cit.

19. "Stanford Facts 2017: The Founding of the University." Stanford University. http://facts.stanford.edu/about/

20. Katherine L. Milkman, Modupe Akinola and Dolly Chugh. "What happens before?" *Journal of Applied Psychology.* Vol 100 (6), 2015.

21. "Atlassian 2017 State of Diversity Report."Atlassian. 2017. https://www.atlassian.com/diversity/survey

22. Castilla, Emilio J. and Stephen Benard. "The Paradox of Meritocracy in Organizations." *Administrative Science Quarterly.* Johnson Graduate School, Cornell University. Vol. 55 (2010). pp. 543-576.

23. Ibid.

24. Pellow, David N. and Park, Lisa Sun-Hee. "The Silicon Valley of Dreams: Environmental Injustice, Immigrant Workers." NYU Press, 22 Dec. 2001.

25. Keyishian, Amy. "Here's Jesse Jackson's Plan for Diversity in Silicon Valley." *Recode.* 14 May 2015. www.recode.net/2015/5/14/11562628/jesse-jackson-has-a-plan-for-diversity-in-silicon-valley

26. See, Silicon Valley Community Foundation at: https://www.siliconvalleycf.org/about-svcf

27. "WASC Self-Study Focus on Learning 2008-2009." Palo Alto High School. http://paly.net/sites/default/files/Paly_WASC_SelfStudy_2008-2009.pdf

28. "Ethnic Responsiveness: Number of organizations that are Culturally and Ethnically Focused." Silicon Valley Indicators. Graph by region. 2010. http://siliconvalleyindicators.org/data/society/arts-culture/ethnic-responsiveness/

29. The Women's Foundation of California. https://womens foundca.org/apply-womens-policy-institute-local-government-2018-19/

30. See, Think of Us at: https://www.thinkof-us.org/about-us/

31. Farley, Shannon. "Nonprofits, not Silicon Valley startups, are creating AI apps for the greater good." *Recode.* 22 June 2017. www.recode.net/2017/6/22/15855492/ai-artificial-intelligence-nonprofit-good-human-chatbots-machine-learning

www.ingramcontent.com/pod-product-compliance
Lightning Source LLC
Chambersburg PA
CBHW030252030426
42336CB00009B/352